Four Prophets Amos Hosea First Isaiah Micah A Modern Translation From The Hebrew

FOUR PROPHETS

Also by J. B. Phillips:

THE NEW TESTAMENT IN MODERN ENGLISH
GOOD NEWS
NEW TESTAMENT CHRISTIANITY
GOD OUR CONTEMPORARY
YOUR GOD IS TOO SMALL
PLAIN CHRISTIANITY
APPOINTMENT WITH GOD
and others

FOUR PROPHETS

AMOS · HOSEA · FIRST ISAIAH · MICAH

*A Modern Translation
from the Hebrew*

by

J. B. PHILLIPS

1963

THE MACMILLAN COMPANY

NEW YORK

Contents

MAPS

THE LAND IN THE TIME OF THE FOUR PROPHETS

THE WORLD SURROUNDING THE FOUR PROPHETS

Translator's Preface

The difficulties of the Hebrew tongue

Many times during the last few years I have found myself wondering why I ever agreed to attempt to translate four Old Testament prophets into the English of today! It is true that scores of well-meaning people from many parts of the world had written urging me, in effect, to do for the Old Testament what I had done for the New. Many hundreds of people, both at public meetings and in private conversation, had asked me to do the same. Of course I was touched and pleased by their confidence in me, but it is extremely difficult to tell people in a few words why Old Testament translation presents such very different problems from those of the New. Apart from the fact that my own knowledge of Hebrew was rather sketchy, I knew intuitively, even before I made any attempt at actual translation, that the task might well prove beyond my powers. I was grateful for an encouraging publisher, and even more grateful for the expert knowledge of Hebrew which the Reverend Edwin Robertson was prepared to put at my disposal. Even so my heart sank at the prospect: perhaps I may explain why.

New Testament Greek, as we should all know by this time, was the common tongue of the Eastern Mediterranean in the days of the Apostles and Evangelists. It is not a particularly polished language, and although it can appear structurally complicated when used in the arguments of St. Paul, it is not beyond our capacities, I think, to grasp its meaning and appreciate its flavour. It is possible to feel at home in such a language. But who could feel at home in the presence of the monolithic grandeur of Old Testament Hebrew? Only, it appeared to me, a chosen few. There seemed to be no concessions to human frailty of understanding in these terse craggy characters. Message after message is packed full of power, and expressed with a terrifying economy of words. I found myself in full agreement with Martin Luther, who once wrote, "The words of the Hebrew tongue have a peculiar energy. It is impossible to convey so much so briefly in any other language. To render them intelligibly we must not attempt to give word for word, but only aim at the sense and the idea."

The matter of the Septuagint

I had thought, in my innocence, that the Septuagint, that translation of the Old Testament into Greek, which was begun in the third century B.C. would lighten my path. But, alas, the practical help that the Septuagint translators could offer me in their version of these four prophets proved very small. Indeed, in the end, I felt bound to discard their version altogether, simply because I found myself growing confused. The Hebrew conveyed to me a meaning which was quite often at variance with the Greek version. No one knows from what Hebrew text the Septuagint scholars worked, but it can hardly have been the same as that which is most widely accepted by scholars today. For the most part I found their Greek perfectly clear and intelligible, but it was baffling and disquieting to find that, when I was facing a real difficulty in the Hebrew, the Greek version provided me with something either quite different, or else—and I hate to say this—with a slick pious phrase.

No Hebrew without tears

So there was no escape, no Hebrew without tears! With every aid that I could lay my hands on I had to come to grips with this forceful language. I wished that those who had so often, and so lightly, said to me, "Why don't you do the Old Testament for us now?", could have shared my feeling of incompetence. I had forgotten that in Hebrew almost every letter is a tensed muscle; I had forgotten that the most menacing diatribe could contain an untranslatable pun; and most certainly I had forgotten that some of the text itself is suspect or defective. Yet there was a challenge about it. I was awed, but I was also fascinated by the sheer authority of this uncompromising tongue.

The question of style

When I translated the letters of the New Testament into modern English my primary concern was to convey the immediacy of their message. In fact I deliberately neglected the intervening centuries and translated the comparatively colloquial Greek into the ordinary English of today. It seemed to me then, and it still seems to me now, that this was the right method for me to use. But I was not unaware that in adopting this "short-circuiting" method I was deliberately destroying any period flavour. To illustrate this point I should like to draw attention to the work of another modern translator, Dr. Hugh Schonfield. Dr. Schonfield is a learned scholar and a Jew, and he entitles his work the *Authentic New Testament*. By giving his book such a title he did not mean to imply that every other translation was in some degree false, but simply that he had attempted to reproduce in his work the authentic Jewish background out of which the New Testament sprang. I am sure he succeeded in this, for no one could read his version without being well aware that he is reading a translation of works written a long time ago; in an utterly different milieu, by people whose traditions and ways of thought were very different from our own. I believe that there is justification for both these methods of approach. As I see it, the important thing to Dr.

Schonfield was to establish historical authenticity; whereas I was prepared to tone down all that was foreign and strange in order to bring across the centuries what I believe to be a timeless message.

Now this difference of approach has a strong bearing upon the problem of how we set about translating the Hebrew of the Old Testament prophets. For the method which I adopted in translating the comparatively simple Greek of *Letters to Young Churches*, for example, was applicable enough to those human, non-literary documents. But it is wildly unsuitable for the transferring into English of the dignified utterance or the passionate pleading of these ancient men of God. There is little hint in any of them of a conversational, let alone a colloquial, style. They were speaking in the name of the Lord and, like King James' translators 2,000 years later, both they and their later editors thought that only the highest language could do justice to the oracles of the Most High.

The limitations of the Authorised Version

In some ways, then, it might be thought that we already possess a version which cannot be surpassed in verbal majesty in the familiar Authorised Version of 1611. But no one could deny that the meaning of even the most beautiful passages is frequently obscure, and the sharp edge of what the prophets had to say is blunted by being enclosed in so beautiful a scabbard. I do not think that we know for certain from what Hebrew sources the translators of 1611 did their work, nor indeed can we even be certain of how sound their knowledge of that difficult language was. But we do know, thanks to the patient work of countless scholars and textual experts of several nations, that today we are much more likely to discover what the prophets actually said. The translators of the Authorised Version can teach us much about the majesty, power and beauty of words. But we must never allow ourselves at any time to be bemused by words, however hallowed or precious. We must, I think, attempt a style at once more lofty than our common speech and yet not so far removed from us that our minds cease to receive the message as God's living Word and relegate it to the realm reserved for aesthetic appreciation. For the Bible was never designed to be read merely as literature. It is the record of God's dealings with men and of the words which some of them spoke in his name.

The question of Hebrew poetry—

We must aim at a style which is both dignified and authoritative. We must somehow indicate the passages which are poetry in Hebrew by breaking up the English into rhythmical lines. I do not think that it is possible to reproduce Hebrew poetry by English poetry, and certainly not by English rhyming verse. We tend to lose more than we gain if we do this, and are apt to produce a light-weight jingle instead of a solemn cadence. The reason for this is not hard to find. Hebrew poetry consists of strong rhythms which are impossible to reproduce in English without destroying the sense. And, although the pun and the play upon words appear to be perfectly acceptable even in the most solemn situation, the idea of rhyme appealed no more to the Hebrew poets than it did to the Greeks or Romans. Next to the rhythm, the most notable characteristic of Hebrew poetry is the *parallelism*—one statement followed by an echoed statement expressed in slightly different words. For example, we probably all remember from the psalms such couplets as:

Praise thè Lord 'O my soul
And all that is within me praise his Holy name.

He will not always chide;
Neither will he keep his anger forever.

Hear my cry O God;
Attend unto my prayer.

or perhaps most familiar of all, because it is used so often in
Anglican churches:

O Lord hear our prayer,
And let our cry come unto thee.

This parallelism is really an equivalent of rhyme. For just
as we may expect to find a rhyme in poetry or verse, and
find it satisfying to the ear, so the Hebrew would be expect-
ing the echo of a thought in the following line. Indeed it is
not very difficult for us to grow accustomed to this form of
verbal "rhyming". We can, therefore, only attempt a com-
promise with Hebrew poetry. We can suggest rhythms and
reproduce parallelisms and use what seems to be the most
suitable language.

—and of Hebrew thought

But of course translation is not as simple as all that.
Hebrew thought is in some ways more distant from us than
either Greek or Latin thought. To take a simple example, we
normally regard the centre of emotion as the heart, though
we can sympathise with the Greeks who could feel compassion in their bowels. But the idea of the *kidneys* instructing us
in the night season (Ps. 16.7) does not strike us very happily.
And the idea that God possesses our kidneys (Ps. 139.13)
does not clearly suggest to our minds the thought that our
whole physical being depends upon God. The fact that the
translators of 1611 used the word "reins" does nothing to
solve the difficulty. And here are a few more examples of the
strangeness of Hebrew idiom. "Cleanness of teeth" (Amos
4.6) does not exactly suggest to us conditions of famine; we
talk of empty mouths or empty bellies. To prophesy that the
people will become a "hissing" (Micah 6.16) does not im-

mediately suggest to us that they will become an object of
scorn and contempt. They should to us be more hissed
against than hissing. We do not normally talk of people "of
unclean lips" (Isaiah 6.5); to us such people are more naturally described as foul-mouthed. Even allowing for poetic
licence it is hard for us to see that murderous hands are
"full of blood" (Isaiah 1.15); to us they are more naturally
dripping with blood. To convey the idea of a human being's
impermanence by saying that "his breath is in his nostrils"
is not very convincing, since we cannot help irreverently
reflecting that a man could always breathe through his
mouth. The meaning of the Hebrew poet can only be conveyed by some such expression as, "who only lives while he
breathes". Further, we are faced again and again with that
favourite Hebrew threat, that someone or something "shall
be cut off". Now this means to us either mutilation, which
is not what is intended, or else (such are our circumstances)
we think of some public supply being disconnected. But it
is extremely difficult to think of a word which conveys the
finality of that decisive Hebrew word.

Some Hebrew poetic expressions have, through the
beauty of the Authorised Version, become part of our own
language. To escape by "the skin of my teeth", to "grind the
faces of the poor", the "four corners of the earth", and the
"Ancient of days" have all been accepted from Hebrew
poetry. Even that very odd expression "as the waters cover
the sea" does not now strike us as foreign. But unless we are
prepared to accept a version which shouts, "translation!" at
every turn, there must be a certain modification of Hebrew
idiom and thought-form. We should be able to know what
the prophet meant and, to some extent, feel what he felt
without being continuously and embarrassingly aware of
that gulf of 2,600 years. In other words, we must try to
place the emphasis on what is of eternal value and tone down
the "accidents" of period and place.

The difficulties of our sources

This is, I believe, the right ideal to pursue in presenting the ancient Word of God to the modern reader, and if we were certain of the original Hebrew manuscripts it would not prove impossible. But unfortunately (and this fact is apparently little known to many devout readers of the Bible) in many instances no one knows for certain what is the original text. Sometimes the text is "defective", which means that some word or words are missing, and sometimes it is "corrupt", which means that later hands have altered, or made additions to, the original writing so that no one now knows what it was. Literally millions of man-hours must have been spent by the experts in comparing and evaluating the available material, and our debt to them is incalculable. And even when their work is, for the moment, done, there remain the frequently conflicting opinions of the commentators.

One example from many

Perhaps one simple illustration will show something of the problem of finding out what the prophet really said.

In Isaiah 15.5 the Authorised Version renders the Hebrew like this:

> My heart shall cry out for Moab; his fugitives shall flee unto Zoar, an heifer of three years old: for by the mounting up of Luhith with weeping shall they go it up; for in the way of Horonaim they shall raise up a cry of destruction.

The Greek Septuagint reads:

> The heart of the Moabitess cries within her towards Segor; for it is a three-year-old heifer. On the ascent of Luhith shall they go up towards you, weeping on the road of Aroniim. She cries, Destruction and an earthquake.

The American Revised Standard Version translates:

My heart cries out for Moab; his fugitives flee to
Eglath-shelishiyah. For at the ascent of Luhith they go up
weeping; on the road to Horonaim they raise a cry of
destruction.

And, Moffat, intelligible as ever:

My soul cries for poor Moab,
as they fly to Zoar
winding their way weeping up to Luhith,
wailing, "We are ruined"

What, we ask in bewilderment, has happened to the three-
year-old heifer? Why did the R.S.V. reproduce that extra-
ordinary polysyllable, Eglath-shelishiyah, without any
explanation?

Is it any wonder that the proper rendering of a single
verse like this may take many hours of reading and thought?

These four Prophets—

For this attempt at translating Hebrew I chose these
prophets, Amos, Hosea, Isaiah and Micah, partly because the
period of their ministry was such a crucial time in the history
of God's chosen people, and partly because they pierce
through a great many falsities (including religious falsities).
Time and again they touch the very heart of the matter—
the way in which men behave towards each other and the
way in which they worship God; and all of these prophets
can see that those two things are inseparable. They are thus,
as it were, clearing the ground for the revolutionary teaching that was to come with the Gospel of Jesus Christ.

The people of Israel had never been so affluent as they
were when Amos attempted rudely to awaken them. But
with prosperity had come inhumanity to man—"the rich
got rich and the poor got poorer"—and the worship of the
false gods of riches, success and security. Moral values had

slumped and even common honesty and decent neighbourliness were being squeezed out by greed and corruption. These four prophets could clearly see this galloping spiritual deterioration, and they not only denounced it but declared in no uncertain terms the consequences of moral and social evil. As prophets they "saw the truth", and as prophets they were constrained to declare what they saw. They were not necessarily foretelling the future, although history proves what remarkably accurate prophets they were in that sense, but they had to warn, even in the most terrifying terms, a people grown deaf and blind to the truth.

—and what they saw

All of these prophetic books include what we might call, if we only read superficially, "a happy ending". But this is because the prophets could see far ahead. As in the "apocalyptic" passages in the synoptic Gospels, or in the Revelation of St. John the Divine, the earthly time-sense is in abeyance. Immediate future and far distant future are equally in focus. I do not myself see any cogent reason for supposing that these visions of a later people returning purified to their own land must be the work "of a later hand". If these prophets could see, with remarkable accuracy, what lay a few years ahead, why not a few hundred or a few thousand years?

But despite their visions, or, if we think more deeply, perhaps because of them, these proclaimers of the truth are solidly down to earth. They will not permit religion to exist in a vacuum. Unless man's worship of God is matched by his just and fair treatment of his neighbour, then ceremonies, rituals, observances and sacrifices are nauseating to God. And they are highly dangerous to the worshipper because he is attempting to stifle his moral and social conscience by all the "business" of religion. He is, in fact, attempting to bribe God. This is what moves all of these prophets, in their different ways, to such violent indignation.

The love of God and the love of man

This declaration of the indissoluble connection between the way in which we love God and the way in which we love our neighbour seems to me unique in the religions of the ancient world. Many religions, though not all, have taught mankind to be merciful and charitable, but the Hebrew prophets are, I believe, alone in declaring the uses of religion to be entirely null and void unless men are treating their fellow men with mercy and justice. To a prophet of the calibre of these men it is not enough to drop a coin into the beggar's palm; you must ask yourself, "*How far am I responsible for his being a beggar at all?*" And this is a thoroughly relevant question today.

This marriage of the love of God and the love of man was the backbone of Christ's teaching seven hundred years later. Sometimes I think we forget that he taught quite categorically that we cannot be forgiven by God unless we also forgive those who injure or offend us. And perhaps not enough notice is taken of the only picture Christ ever painted of the last Judgment, recorded in the twenty-fifth chapter of St. Matthew's Gospel. Here it is most plainly stated that the way we treat our fellows is an exact replica of the way in which we are treating the Son of God himself—surely a piercing and devastating truth if ever there was one! I am myself not over-blessed with a historical sense, but I am amazed that these bold men were declaring such vital truth in the days of Homer, long before the hey-day of Athens, and when Rome, the so-called "eternal city", was little more than a village.

They speak with authority

Despite the distance in time, the frequent unfamiliarity of idiom and the imperfect state of the Hebrew text, these four men speak with uncommon authority. All four strongly convey the sense that they are seeing the truth about God and man. There is something peculiarly compelling about men who have the deepest possible reverence for God and yet can say, "This is what the Lord says."

In these books there are some crude anthropomorphisms which offend our modern minds, and, naturally, the conception of God is a pre-Christian one. Nevertheless we are left with an overwhelming conviction that God is God, right is right and wrong is wrong; and that in itself is an iron tonic to us moderns. For most of us today are afraid of denouncing evil for fear of being called intolerant; we are not allowed to be morally indignant for "psychology says" that what is making us angry is an identical fault in ourselves! We are not allowed to have any definite values of right and wrong, for all things, we are told, are purely relative—though relative to *what* is not made clear. In these days we can scarcely spare a thought for the victim of vicious assault for all our sympathy is needed for the brutal and callous aggressor. We are frightened of sharing our faith with a fellow human being for fear of interfering with the sanctity of his private beliefs; we are even scared of living out the principles of the Gospel lest we are labelled contemptuously as "do-gooders".

But here in this world of nearly three thousand years ago human beings are far less self-conscious. They can be noble, wise, brave and good, but they can also be cruel, stupid, greedy, fickle or just plain wicked. We are back in a world of real people, potentially sons and daughters of the Most High, but making tragically wrong choices and treating each other abominably. But these four prophets assume always that men have consciences and that they have the power to choose their path. If they are beyond the reach of messages of sweetness and light, then violent, indeed terrifying, threats and warnings must be used to crack their dreadful complacency.

These men were not in the least concerned to make their

message "acceptable". They were not out to placate the people in power or to conciliate the clever; their whole purpose was to speak "the word of the Lord". Such voices of integrity, despite all the obscurities and difficulties of the text, still sound like a trumpet down the centuries.

It seems to me (and Heaven knows any honest man can observe this in his own spirit) that human beings are forever trying to evade moral responsibility, while God is eternally trying to make them accept it, and thus grow up into being his sons. Because of this human tendency the world of the Bible is bound to be an uncomfortable world. For here God, not man, is master. Here God speaks and man, if he is wise, will listen with a proper humility.

The need for commentary

I have said more than once that a translator is not a commentator; his job is communication. I have done my best to translate, not for the scholar but for the ordinary intelligent layman. I have tried, wherever possible, without distorting the Hebrew, to convey the Prophets' message as clearly as I can. Yet I feel I must say that no one is going to get the best out of these four prophets without the help of some expert interpreter.

I therefore recommend the following:

The relevant sections in William Neil's *One Volume Bible Commentary*, published by Hodder & Stoughton.

The Torch Commentaries on these books, published by the Student Christian Movement.

For those who want fuller treatment, there are books on these prophets in The Cambridge Bible Series; and the commentaries by George Adam Smith, published by Hodder & Stoughton in the *Expositor's Bible*, are excellent.

For the fullest, most complete and scholarly commentary, there are the appropriate volumes on these prophets in the series called The International Critical Commentary, published by T. & T. Clark. Unfortunately in the really magnificent commentary on Isaiah, the book stops short at chapter 27. It stopped there in 1911, and I much hope the publishers will see fit to complete a task so competently begun.

I would also recommend the work, which is both translation and commentary on Isaiah, of the Roman Catholic scholar Monsignor Edward J. Kissane, published by Browne and Nolan.

There is also the beautifully-produced *Interpreter's Bible* published by the Abingdon Press. The section dealing with Isaiah is particularly valuable, as account is taken of some better readings made available through the Dead Sea Scrolls.

The new *Peake's Commentary*, published by Nelson, was not available until my translation was nearly finished. I did not use it then, but subsequent reading of it makes me recommend it warmly.

Cross-headings, etc.

In my work of translating I have used cross-headings to break up solid masses of words since I began writing *Letters to Young Churches* in 1941. Many people appreciate them; a few detest them. To those whom they annoy, may I suggest that they ignore them? It will be noticed that the cross-headings are very simply worded, indeed in some cases they are what Mr. Punch used to call "glimpses of the obvious"! This is deliberate, for, as I said above, it is not my job to make comment or to lead the reader into some conclusion which may be merely my own opinion. There are some gaps without cross-headings; these are places where the thought is abruptly changed but any comment of mine would be bound to be tendentious.

After some consideration my publisher and I decided to include verse numbers, albeit unobtrusively. This is for the

TRANSLATOR'S PREFACE

benefit of students or schoolchildren who may be studying
these prophets and need to find their way about quickly.
But it is hoped that this will not interfere with the fairly
fast reading through of several chapters at a time, which is
often necessary to get the feel and sweep of the prophet's
heart and mind. In a few cases verses are replaced in what I
think, after very careful thought, is more likely to be the
original order. In a very few cases a verse has been dropped
altogether because our improved knowledge of the manuscripts, not forgetting the evidence of the Dead Sea Scrolls,
enables us to see where a copyist, unknowingly in all prob-
ability, repeated a verse, or simply made a small human
error. These changes are obvious from the re-arrangement of
verse numbers.

Acknowledgements

Any translator, especially one who attempts the books of
the Old Testament where the text is doubtful, owes a great
deal to the textual critics and to the commentators. I have
learned much from many scholars as I have made this translation, and it would be impossible to name them all. But I
am sincerely grateful to them, and especially to the Reverend
Edwin Robertson, who has scrupulously perused every word
of my work and made the most useful comments. I must
make it quite clear, however, that he is not responsible for
the final choices that I made. I am particularly grateful
to him for supplying the Historical Background which
gives the proper setting to these urgent and moving
messages.

Apart from my wife, who throughout this task has been
secretary, collaborator and critic, I must also thank my sister,
Mrs. Thornton Weekley, for her help in the laborious business of typing and re-typing, checking and re-checking as
well as for proof-reading. Mrs. Weekley also spent many
hours preparing the rough drawings from which the maps
were made.

Finally I must thank my friend and publisher Jocelyn Gibb, who has been the soul of patience during the two years and more, which this work has taken to complete. He has been full of useful suggestions and stimulating encouragements and has never menaced me with a dead-line!

J. B. PHILLIPS

Swanage 1963

Historical Background

by

E. H. ROBERTSON

There are times in human history when all the world
seems astir. A wind blows through human affairs which cannot be easily explained by the normal channels of communication. In popular parlance, we say that "something is
in the air". A few years ago Mr. Macmillan, the Prime
Minister of Britain, described a similar phenomenon in
Africa as "a wind of change". Europe in 1848 felt the stir-
ring of revolution, from Karl Marx in the British Museum
to the turbulence of Central Europe and the insights of
Kierkegaard. But one of the greatest stirrings in human history was in the century with which this book is concerned,
approximately 750–650 B.C. It can be detected from Cornwall to China.

As the Middle Bronze Age came to an end, Cornwall, so
far almost isolated, began to feel the pressures of Celtic civilisation. It was in this century, the central part of what Karl
Jaspers has called the "axle period" of human history, that
Celtic refugees, pressed out of their homelands on the con-
tinent, and poured into Cornwall as far west as Land's End.
They made full use of the Cornish tin mines and brought
prosperity and culture. They brought the tools that made the
Bronze Age flower and skills that gave improved shapes to
weapons, tools and utensils: a leaf-shaped spear, a double-
headed slashing sword, a circular shield, a socketed-axe,
punches, small anvils, chisels, saws, sickles and ploughshares.

Much the same was happening at the other end of
Europe. The lake dwellers of Lake Constance had turned

their dull existence into the beginning of a cultured civilisation. Anyone who has visited that fascinating reconstruction of the villages of lake dwellers which lies opposite the island of Mainau, at Unteruhldingen, will have noted the startling difference effected by this century of change. The life depicted in the dim, undecorated houses of the earlier period bears no comparison with the richly varied and artistic life shown in the later village, constructed during this "axle period". The name is a good one. History turned round, like a wheel round its axle, during this hundred years and began to move in a new direction.

Greece had not yet reached the glory of fifth-century Athens but Homer was writing and had already fashioned a language and a series of models for the greater dramatists. Pericles had not yet built the Parthenon, but the skills he needed and even the artistic forms had their origin in the eighth century. There have been many theories about the writing of the *Iliad* and the *Odyssey* but it seems clear that Homer covers the names of many poets. All that can be said with certainty is that, among the many sources, the oldest come in the period 750–650 B.C. The wind blowing through the world fanned a spark of genius into the origins of European civilisation.

Moving further east, we touch the lands of the first four writing prophets. They were the tiny countries of Israel and Judah, surrounded by quarrelsome neighbours and crushed between world empires. This was the period of Assyria's great expansion and culture, as excavations constantly confirm, and it was the military exploits of this great empire which form the backcloth to the prophets' words. Her power to crush was seen as the instrument of divine anger and this period saw terrible examples of its use. Egypt, constantly denounced by these prophets, as "a broken reed", untrustworthy, was no decadent power, as the most casual visit to Egypt can confirm. This was the century of Assyria's might and Egypt's culture. Further east the wind still blew.

Zoroaster had not yet appeared on the Persian scene but he was probably born towards the end of this period, about 650 B.C. A characteristic of this century everywhere was that it prepared the way for great events. Just as those four early prophets gave warning of much to come and prepared the way for later prophecies of great beauty, like the Servant Songs of a later Isaiah, the pathos of Jeremiah and the rich imagery of Ezekiel, so in other parts of the world the wind stirred to life, but did not fashion to finished splendour. The preparatory character of the growth in Greece has already been mentioned. It was the same in Persia. We know little about the period before Zoroaster came as a refugee but it is clear that the soil was well prepared for the growth of his teaching. The great battle between the powers of God and the powers of Evil could be dramatically portrayed against the Persian scene of this period. History seemed to be proving Zoroaster right. So deeply did his teaching root itself in the hearts of the people, that centuries later, Zoroastrians in large numbers escaped to the freedom of India when Moslem rule was imposed. The Parsees of today bear witness to the tenacious faith that needed no native soil to sustain it. But there were no Parsees yet in India nor Zoroastrians in Persia when Amos was silenced at Bethel. But the wind that sent him back to record his words in the solitude of Tekoa, blew also over the plains of India. In this period the Upanishads were written and Hinduism was blossoming, in preparation again for the great reforming movement of Buddhism. But for the changes that took place in Hinduism during this century, Buddhism would have found no nourishment a century later. Even in distant China the wind that saw its results in Confucius and the Taoism of Laotse, blew steadily.

Over the whole world the Spirit of God stirred the spirit of man. In Judah and Israel four men spoke in the name of the living God, conscious of why they spoke. They knew nothing of the world movement but they were at the heart of it. Small and insignificant as Israel and Judah were, their geographical position gave them a grandstand view of world history and at times the game entered their box. The prophets were not political commentators, but they saw world events as evidence of God's power in the world. They also believed that the whole of history was to serve his purpose in preparing his people. Thus their real interest was Israel or Judah, not world powers like Assyria or Egypt. They urged God's people to obey God's laws and promised great things if they did. Egypt and Assyria were just examples of powers that would bow before them. They warned God's people of the consequences of disobeying God's commands or living lives unworthy of the people of God. Again, Egypt and Assyria were used as examples. Their power illustrated the power of God and they would be used to punish God's people. Even if they were much wickeder than Israel, they could still be used by God to punish. Their turn would come later.

The great historical event which gave colour to the prophetic warning of this period was the fall of Samaria in 732 B.C. when the whole of the North, Syria and Israel, was depopulated and organised as Assyrian provinces. Amos had warned of this and it had come to pass. The terrible events sobered Judah and her prophets, particularly Isaiah, were listened to. The general line taken by the prophets was trust in God and keep out of foreign alliances. It was good for Judah's morals and also sound political advice. As a result Judah survived this dangerous century. Later, she interpreted her good fortune as a security guaranteed by the presence of the Temple in Jerusalem. As soon as magical confidence took the place of true religion, the seeds of destruction began to germinate. Eventually, even Jerusalem fell. But the prophets had seen beyond this and had taught a survival of God's people beyond disaster. Their teaching has kept the Jewish people intact despite the centuries of persecution.

This book contains a modern translation of all that remains

of the writing of these four prophets who had little in common except that they all spoke Hebrew, believed that what they declared was the Word of God to their people and their utterances were made at the turning point of ancient history. After this century, history took a new turn and we live in the aftermath and results of their words, spoken at the dawn of an age which was to include the coming of Jesus Christ and all the great religions of the world as we know them. No written material of any lasting religious significance survives from the period before these eighth-century prophets.

E. H. R.

The Book of Amos

The Book of Amos

THE PROPHET. *Amos is the earliest of the four prophets; his was a short sharp ministry, exercised in about 755 B.C. Nothing is known of his family history, and we only know on the evidence of the book itself that he had been a shepherd in the howling wilderness of Tekoa, and that he tended sycamore trees. Amos was a countryman, called not by some vision, such as Isaiah was given, but by a burning sense of moral righteousness and social justice. He was not a sensitive or emotional man like Hosea; he was stern, austere and uncompromising. We can imagine him, as he preached in Israel at Bethel, the centre of religion but also of luxurious corruption, as rather like a hard Calvinist from remoter Scotland confronted by the worldliness and luxury of London, New York or Paris. The fact that Amos lacked sympathetic hearing, and was officially denounced by the priest Amaziah, probably made the tenor of his message harsher than ever.*

THE THEME. *The prophecies of the Book of Amos are of almost unrelieved gloom. He can see clearly that the softness and corruption at the heart of Israel will make her fall an easy prey to the invader. The future is so clear to the prophet that he sees the Assyrians advancing to the attack some years before they did in fact set out.*

To Amos, God was the Lord God of hosts, a Sovereign who ruled the heavens as well as the earth, nature and all nations. In the prophet's eyes God's chosen people do not have a monopoly, so to speak, of the one true God. It is true that God has established a special relationship with them, but on this account he will judge them the more strictly.

It should be remembered that these messages of denunciation were delivered in an atmosphere of unprecedented material prosperity, accompanied by a widespread decay of moral values and a

3

wicked oppression of the poor. Disaster seemed most unlikely, yet within a very few years four kings of Israel had been assassinated, then Hoshea was deposed and imprisoned and Israel ceased to be a nation.

The only note of hope in this book seems to be in the far future, when God's judgements and punishments are over and the nation is restored to its own land.

CHAPTER ONE

The Prophet's message

1 These are the words of Amos when he saw the truth about Israel. At that time he lived among the men who tend the small sheep of Tekoa. Uzziah was king of Judah and Jeroboam, the son of Joash, was king of Israel, and it was two years before the earthquake.

The Lord speaks in judgement—

2 This is what the Lord says:
The Lord roars from Zion,
And thunders out of Jerusalem,
So that the pasture-lands are blighted,
And the green ridge of Carmel withers.

—against Damascus

3 This is what the Lord says:
Because of outrage after outrage committed by Damascus
I will not relent!
For they have battered Gilead,
They have threshed her with iron-studded sledges,
4 And for this I will destroy the power of the house of Hazael,
And overthrow the rulers in Ben-hadad.

4

5 I will smash the defences of Damascus,
I will wipe out the people of the Aven valley,
And the sceptred king from Beth-eden.
The people of Syria shall go captive to Kir—
By order of the Lord!

—against Philistia

6 This is what the Lord says:
Because of outrage after outrage committed by Gaza
I will not relent!
For they carried off an entire population
To sell them as slaves to Edom.

7 And for this I will destroy the power of Gaza,
And overthrow her rulers.

8 I will wipe out the people of Ashdod,
And the sceptred king from Ashkelon.
I will strike my blows against Ekron
Until the last Philistine is dead—
By order of the Lord God!

—against Tyre

9 This is what the Lord says:
Because of outrage after outrage committed by Tyre
I will not relent!
For they sold a whole population to Edom
And forgot the ties of brotherhood.

10 For this I will destroy the power of Tyre,
And overthrow her rulers.

—against Edom

11 This is what the Lord says:
Because of outrage after outrage committed by Edom
I will not relent!

For he pursued his brother with a sword in his hand.
He stifled compassion, nursed the anger in his heart,
And cherished his fury.
12 For this I will destroy the power of Teman,
And overthrow the rulers in Bozrah.

—against Ammon

13 This is what the Lord says:
Because of outrage after outrage committed by the
    Ammonites
I will not relent!
For when they extended their frontiers
They ripped up pregnant women in Gilead.
14 For this I will destroy the power of Rabbah,
And overthrow her rulers.
With cries of death on the battle-field
And the roaring blast of a storm,
15 Their king shall go into exile—
He and his nobles together—
By order of the Lord!

CHAPTER TWO

—against Moab

1 This is what the Lord says:
Because of outrage after outrage committed by Moab
I will not relent!
For he burned to lime the bones of the dead king of
    Edom.
2 Therefore, I will destroy the power of Moab,
And overthrow the rulers in Kerioth,
And Moab shall die in an uproar of shouting and the
    sound of trumpets.
3 I will destroy her king,

6

And kill all her princes with him—
By order of the Lord!

—against Judah

4　This is what the Lord says:
Because of outrage after outrage committed by Judah
I will not relent!
For they have spurned the Word of the Lord
And failed to keep his commandments.
The very idols which led their fathers astray
Have deceived them also.
5　Therefore, I will destroy the power of Judah,
And overthrow the rulers in Jerusalem.

—against Israel

6　This is what the Lord says:
Because of outrage after outrage committed by Israel
I will not relent!
For they have sold the innocent for a handful of
　　silver,
And needy men for a pair of shoes.
7　They grind the faces of the poor into the dust,
And force the humble out of his rightful path.
Father and son use the same temple-girl,
And so defile my holy name.
8　Beside every altar they lounge on garments which they
　　took in pledge,
And in the houses of their gods they drink away the
　　money they imposed in fines.

The Lord's stern reminder

9　Yet it was I who destroyed the Amorite before your eyes,
A man as tall as cedar and strong as oak.

But I destroyed his fruit above the ground, and his roots
  below.
And that you might inherit the land of the Amorite,

10   It was I who brought you up out of the land of Egypt,
And led you in the wilderness for forty years.

11   It was I, too, who raised up some of your sons to be
  prophets,
And some of your young men to be Nazirites.
Is this not true, you children of Israel?
This is the Lord himself speaking to you.

12   But you forced the Nazirites to drink wine,
And forbade the prophets to prophesy.

The Lord's inescapable punishment

13   Look, I will make you groan in your tracks beneath my
  weight,
As the sheaf-covered earth groans beneath the weight of
  the loaded cart!

14   Swiftness of foot will prove no escape,
The strong man's strength will avail him nothing,
And the fighting man will not escape alive.

15   The archer will not stand his ground,
And the fleet of foot will not run clear,
Nor will the horseman make his escape.

16   In that day the bravest warrior will take to his heels,
And run away, stripped and unarmed!
This is the order of the Lord.

CHAPTER THREE

The Lord's indictment of his people

1 Listen, you people of Israel, to the charge which the Lord
brings against you—against the whole nation which I brought
up out of the land of Egypt!

2 You only have I chosen from all the nations of the earth.
Therefore it is you whom I will punish for all your wrong-
doings.

The Prophet foresees Israel's doom

3 Can two walk together unless they have agreed to do so?
4 Does a lion roar in the forest when there is no prey for
him,
Or the young lion growl in his lair if he has made no kill?
5 Does a bird fall to the ground unless it is caught?
Does the trap fly up when there is no bird to catch?
6 And do not the people of the city tremble when the alarm
is sounded?
Can a city suffer disaster unless the Lord is its cause?
7 Surely the Lord God does nothing without showing his
purpose to his servants the prophets!
8 When the lion roars who is not afraid?
When the Lord God speaks who can fail to prophesy?

The evils of Samaria

9 Now make a proclamation to all the palaces in Assyria,
And the palaces in the land of Egypt, and say,
Gather together on the hill of Samaria,
And see the dreadful disorders there,
How oppression flourishes in her heart.
10 They have forgotten how to do right, says the Lord.

9

They maintain their palaces by the fruit of violence and
    robbery.

The pronouncement of her doom

11   Therefore the Lord God says this:
    The land shall be overwhelmed by disaster
    And your strength shall be stripped from you,
    While all your palaces shall be plundered.

12   The Lord says this:
    As a shepherd may snatch from the mouth of a lion
    No more than two bits of bone or a torn piece of an ear,
    So shall the children of Israel be rescued—
    All that will be left of Samaria will be a scrap of couch
    Or a tattered piece of pillow.

The Lord's coming punishment

13   Listen and bear witness against the house of Jacob,
    Says the Lord God, the God of hosts.

14   On the day that I punish Israel for his iniquities
    I will visit the very altars of Bethel,
    And the horns of the altar shall be struck
    And will fall to the ground.

15   I will strike both winter-house and summer-house.
    The ivory-panelled houses will be destroyed,
    And the great mansions shall be no more—
    By order of the Lord!

CHAPTER FOUR

Women who love luxury—

1 Listen to this charge, you cows of Bashan,
Women who glitter on the heights of Samaria,
Who defraud the poor, and ride roughshod over the
  needy,
While you keep ordering your husbands,
Bring us wine to drink!

—will suffer a terrible doom

2 The Lord God swears by his glory
That your day is coming,
The day when you will be dragged out with hooks,
The last of you with fish-hooks.
3 And every one of you will be dragged headlong
Through gaps in the walls made by your enemies,
And you will be transported to Harmon—
By order of the Lord!

An ironic message to the people

4 Go on, then, to Bethel, and get on with your sinning;
Go to Gilgal, and pile up your sins.
5 Yes, bring your sacrifices every morning,
And pay your tithes every third day;
Burn your bread as a thank-offering,
Advertise your free-will gifts,
Be sure everyone hears of them!
For this is what you love to do, you children of Israel.
These are the words of the Lord God.

The Lord's disasters have not changed Israel

6   It was I who gave you hungry mouths in all your cities,
And famine throughout the land,
And yet, says the Lord, you have not returned to me.

7   Yes, I stopped the rain from falling three months before
the harvest.
I sent rain on one city and withheld it from another;
One field would get its rain while the rainless field would
wither.

8   Two or three cities staggered to another city to drink
water,
But they never had enough.
Yet, says the Lord, you have not returned to me.

9   I struck you with blight and mildew,
I scorched your gardens and your vineyards;
Locusts devoured your figs and your olive-trees,
And yet, says the Lord, you have not returned to me.

10   I sent an Egyptian plague upon you.
While your horses were captured
I cut down your young men with the sword;
And I made the stench of your camps fill your nostrils.
And yet, says the Lord, you have not returned to me.

11   I overthrew some of your cities,
As Sodom and Gomorrah were overthrown,
Till you were like charred sticks snatched from the blaze.
And yet, says the Lord, you have not returned to me.

Israel must prepare to meet God

12   Therefore this is something which I will do to you, Israel,
And because I am going to do this thing
Make yourselves ready to meet your God, Israel.

13   Remember it is the One who forms the mountains and
creates the wind,
The One who explains Man's thoughts to man,

The One who turns dawn into darkness,
And strides upon the high places of the earth—
And the Lord, the God of hosts, is his name!

CHAPTER FIVE

The Prophet mourns over Israel

1 Listen while I denounce you,
   And hear this funeral dirge, you house of Israel!
2 The virgin Israel shall fall to rise no more—
   Deserted on her own soil, with none to lift her up.

God's warning

3 This is what the Lord God says:
   The city which goes forth a thousand strong
   Will return with a mere hundred;
   And the city which goes forth a hundred strong,
   Will return to the house of Israel with only ten.

God's advice

4 This is what the Lord says to the house of Israel:
   Seek me and live.
5 Do not seek Bethel, the House of God,
   Nor go to Gilgal, nor cross over to Beer-sheba.
   For Gilgal shall know the gall of exile,
   And the House of God will have lost its meaning.

Fear the Lord—

6 Seek the Lord and live—
   Lest he break out like fire, you house of Joseph,
   A fire which burns and burns, which no one at Bethel can
      quench.

13

7 Listen to this, you who have made justice a bitter jest,
And integrity of no account!

—and remember his power

8 He who made the starry universe,
Who turns darkness into morning light,
And darkens the day into nightfall,
Who summons the waters of the sea,
And pours them out upon the face of the earth,
This is the One whose name is the Lord;
9 He it is who flings ruin in the face of the strong,
And rains destruction upon the fortress.

Evil men will not flourish

10 They hate the honest witness in the court,
And loathe the man of integrity.
11 Therefore, because you trample on the weak,
And compel him to give you loads of grain,
You may have built stone houses,
But they will never be your home.
You have planted vineyards for your own pleasure,
But you will never drink their wine.
12 For I know how wilful are your crimes,
And how determined are your sins—
You browbeat honest men, you take bribes,
And ignore the poor man's claim for justice.
13 Therefore a wise man keeps his mouth shut,
For the days are full of menace.

The only way out

14 Seek good and not evil—
There is no life for you otherwise,
And you will never find that the Lord, the God of hosts,

14

Is with you, as you say he is.
15   Yes, loathe evil and love good,
Set justice on her feet again;
And then it may be that the Lord, the God of hosts,
Will have pity upon what remains of Joseph.

But if evil is persisted in—

16   Therefore the Lord, the God of hosts, the Lord himself
     says:
There shall be wailing in every courtyard,
And cries of woe in all your streets.
Farm-workers shall be called to join the mourning,
And wailers will be hired to lead the lamentation.
17   Even in the vineyards there shall be wailing,
When I sweep through your land, says the Lord.

—the day of the Lord will mean calamity

18   Alas for those who long for the day of the Lord!
Why long for such a day?
The day of the Lord will be a day of darkness, not a day
     of light.
19   It will be like a man running from a lion,
Only to find himself clutched by a bear.
Like a man who runs into his own home,
And as he leans his hand against the wall
Is bitten by a snake.
20   Is it not true that the day of the Lord
Will be darkness and not light,
Pitch-darkness with no brightening gleam?

God requires inner integrity

21   I loathe and despise your festivals;
Your meetings for sacrifice give me no pleasure.

15

22 You may bring me your burnt-offerings, your meal-
    offerings,
    Or your thank-offerings of fat cattle,
    And I shall not so much as look at them.
23 Let me have no more of your noisy hymns;
    My ears are closed to the music of your harps.
24 Instead, let justice roll on like a mighty river,
    And integrity flow like a never-failing stream!

Look back to the days of simple trust

25 Was it sacrifices and gifts that you brought me all those forty
26 years in the desert, you house of Israel? But now you must
    bear the burden of Sakkuth your king, and Kaiwan your
27 star-god—idols which you have made for yourselves. And I
    will send you away into exile far beyond Damascus. The
    Lord, whose name is the God of hosts, has spoken.

CHAPTER SIX

A complacent present leads to a disastrous future

1 Alas for the complacent ones in Zion,
   Who live on the heights of Samaria without a care,
   Appointed leaders of the foremost nation,
   Respected by the whole house of Israel!
2 Cross over to Calneh and look at it.
   Go from there to great Hamath,
   And then go down to Gath of the Philistines.
   Are you any better than these kingdoms?
   Or is your land any greater than theirs?
3 You put off the day of reckoning,
   Yet bring ever nearer the days of misrule!
4 You who lie on beds of ivory,
   And sprawl upon your couches,
   Eating choice lamb and farm-fed veal.

16

5 Who croon to the music of the harp,
And compose melodies as though you were David himself!

6 You who drink wine by the bowl-full,
And anoint yourselves with the finest oils.
But never a thought do you spare
For the terrible miseries of Joseph!

7 For these very reasons you will be the first to go into
exile,
While the revelry of the dissolute shall die away—
By order of the Lord, the God of hosts!

The Lord's anger against pride—

8 The Lord has sworn by himself,
I detest the pride of Jacob,
And I loathe his gorgeous palaces.
I will abandon his city and all that is in it.

—and his punishment

9 This will be the way of it: if there are ten men left in a house,
10 they shall die. And if some kinsman comes with the body-
burner to take the body out of the house to burn it, and calls
out to anyone hiding in the far corners of the house, Is there
anyone left with you? He will answer, No one; and the
burner will say, Hush! There will be no help from God.

11 See, the Lord has commanded that the great house shall
be utterly destroyed,
And the small house smashed to pieces.

God's Laws cannot be flouted

12 Can horses race over rocks?
Can you plough the sea with oxen?

17

Yet you make justice a deadly poison,
And a life of honesty a bitter thing;
13 You, who are so proud of what has no being,
And boast that you have grown strong by efforts of your
own.
Look, you house of Israel,
14 I am raising up a nation against you,
Says the Lord, the God of hosts.
And they shall crush you from the pass of Hamath
To the river-bed of Arabah.

CHAPTER SEVEN

The threat of locusts

1 Then the Lord God made me see this sight:
There he was, preparing a locust swarm—
It was after the king's mowing had been taken,
And the main crop was growing up—
2 And as the locusts began to devour the whole green
growth, I cried.
Have mercy, Lord, have mercy!
How can Jacob withstand this?
He is so small.
3 Then the Lord relented,
And the Lord said, This shall not be.

The threat of drought

4 Then the Lord God made me see this sight:
There he was, calling for a trial by fire,
To dry up the deep springs of water.
5 It had begun to scorch the land, when I said,
O Lord God, stop this, I pray!
How can Jacob withstand it?
He is so small.

6   Then the Lord relented,
    And the Lord God said, This too shall not happen.

The Lord's true judgement

7   Then the Lord made me see this sight:
    There he was, standing beside a wall
    With a plumb-line in his hand.

8   Then the Lord said to me,
    What do you see, Amos?
    And I said, A plumb-line.
    And the Lord replied,
    See, I test my people Israel by the straightness of this
      line,
    And I will not relent again.

9   For Isaac's high places shall be razed to the ground,
    The shrines of Israel reduced to ruin,
    And I will draw the sword against the house of Jero-
      boam.

The Prophet denounced by the priest

10 Then Amaziah the priest of Bethel, sent a message to Jero-
    boam, king of Israel, saying, Amos is conspiring against you,
    in the very heart of Israel. The people cannot bear what he
11 is saying, for Amos has declared:

    Jeroboam shall die by the sword,
    And Israel must go into exile,
    Far from her own country.

12 Then Amaziah said to Amos:
    Get out, you silly dreamer! Run away to Judah,
    Earn your bread and make your prophecies there.

13 You shall no longer prophesy at Bethel—
    Here is the king's holy place, and here his royal palace!

The Prophet's devastating reply

14 Then Amos replied to Amaziah: I am neither a prophet nor
the son of a prophet—I am a shepherd and I tend sycamore
15 trees. But it was the Lord who took me from herding my
little sheep, and it was the Lord who said to me, Go and
prophesy against my people Israel.

16   Now therefore, hear the word of the Lord!
    You say to me, Do not prophesy against Israel,
    And speak no word against the house of Isaac.
17   Therefore the Lord says this:
    Your wife shall be ravished in the public street;
    Your daughters and your sons shall be killed by the
        sword.
    Your land shall be divided up into pieces,
    And you yourself shall die upon pagan soil!
    And Israel shall surely go into exile,
    Far from her own land.

CHAPTER EIGHT

A nation ripe for disaster

1 Then the Lord God made me see this sight. there was a
2 basket full of ripe fruit. And he said, Amos what do you see?
And I said, A basket full of ripe fruit. Then the Lord said
to me,

    So are my people Israel ripe for destruction.
    I will not relent again.

God does not overlook man's inhumanity to man

4   Listen to this, you who trample upon the needy,
    And grind the faces of the poor!

5   You who say, When will the new moon be past,
So that we may sell our grain?
When will the sabbath be over,
So that we may offer our corn for sale?
While you make your measure short
And your prices high,
And cheat with biased scales.

6   And all to possess the poor for silver,
And the needy for the price of a pair of shoes,
Selling for grain the sweepings from your floor.

7   The Lord has sworn by the glory of Jacob,
Never will I forget what you have done.

8   Because of it, shall not the earth be made to quake,
And every inhabitant of it to mourn?
Shall not the whole land rise like the Nile,
And sink like Egypt's flood?

The consequence will be darkness, death and despair

9   On that day, the Lord God declares,
I will make the sun go down at noon
And darken the earth in broad daylight.

3   In that day the singing in the temple will be turned to
wailing,
Says the Lord God,
As everywhere corpse is thrown upon corpse in deathly
silence.

10   I will turn your feasts into funerals
And your songs into dirges.
I will put sackcloth upon every man's loins,
And every man's head shall be shaved in mourning.
I will make your mourning like the lament for an only
son,
And the end of it will be bitter despair.

The ultimate famine—the loss of God's Word

11　See, the days are coming, says the Lord God,
When I will send a famine on the land.
It will not be a famine of bread or water,
But of hearing the words of the Lord.

12　Men shall wander from sea to sea,
They shall run to and fro,
From the north to the east,
Seeking the Word of the Lord,
But they shall not find it.

13　In that day fair maidens and young men
Shall faint and fall—

14　Those who swear by the god of Samaria,
Who say, As your god lives, O Dan,
And swear by the way of Beer-sheba—
They shall fall and never rise again!

CHAPTER NINE

There is no escape from the Lord

1　I saw the Lord standing above the altar, and he said,
Strike the tops of the pillars till the foundations shake.
Yes, break them down upon the heads of them all!
The last of them I will strike with the sword.
Not one of them shall get clear away;
There will be no survivors!

2　If they dug through to the land of the Dead,
My hand would catch them.
If they climbed up into the heavens,
I would drag them down.

3　If they hid in the topmost peak of Carmel,
I would find them and bring them out.
If they were to hide from me in the depths of the sea,
I would command Leviathan to crush them in his jaws.

22

4   If they went into exile under the eyes of their enemies,
     I would command the sword, and it would slay them.
     My eye will be upon them for evil and not for good.

Remember the power of the Lord

5   This is the Lord, God of hosts.
     He has but to touch the earth for it to melt,
     And all its inhabitants cry out in fear,
     While the whole earth rises like the Nile,
     And sinks like the floods of Egypt.
6   He is the One who builds his palaces in the heavens,
     And makes his domed arch rest firmly upon the earth.
     The One who summons the waters of the sea,
     And pours them over the land—
     His name is the Lord.

The Lord sees all nations—

7   Are you not the same to me, says the Lord,
     As the Ethiopians, you men of Israel?
     Was it not I who brought up Israel
     Out of the land of Egypt;
     And did I not bring the Philistines from Caphtor,
     And the Assyrians from Kir?
8   See, the eyes of the Lord God
     Are watching the sinful kingdom,
     And I will wipe it off the face of the earth.
     Nevertheless, I will not utterly destroy the house of
       Jacob.
     It is the Lord who declares this.

—but Israel should not be complacent

9   See, I, the Lord, am commanding that the house of Israel
     Be shaken among all the nations,

Like grain shaken in a sieve.
Not one good kernel falls to the ground
Of all my sinful people.

10 All those who say, Disaster will never touch us
And can never threaten our security,
Shall be killed with the sword.

Yet the day of restoration will come—

11 In that day, I will raise the fallen tent of David,
And repair its damage.
I will raise his ruins,
And rebuild them as in the days of old,
12 So that the people may possess what is left of Edom,
And of all the nations which belong to me.
It is the Lord who will do this and who now declares it.

—with prosperity and security

13 The days are coming, the Lord declares,
When the ploughman will overtake the reaper,
And he who treads the grapes will overtake the sower.
When the mountains are wet with new wine,
And the hills grow soft with it.
14 That will be when I bring back
The exiles of my people Israel,
To rebuild deserted cities and live in them,
To plant vineyards and drink their wine,
To make gardens and eat their fruit.
15 And I will plant them in their own land.
Never again shall they be uprooted
From the land which I gave to them.
The Lord, your God, has spoken.

The Book of Hosea

The Book of Hosea

THE PROPHET. *Unlike Amos, who descended upon the Northern Kingdom from his home in Judah, Hosea is a native of Israel and writes from within the situation which Amos so terribly foretold. He begins his prophecies a few years after the message of the older prophet. The disasters have already begun, and Hosea speaks as a daily observer of Israel's unfaithfulness and corruption, of her vacillations and her obstinacy. He is plainly a man of feeling and passion. His own personal tragedy leads him to a far deeper understanding of the nature of forgiving and redeeming love. Yet it is not always clear whether the prophet's experience with Gomer is teaching him about God, or whether he is learning about his wife from his understanding of Israel. The two run on parallel lines and flash a meaning across to each other.*

THE THEME. *The general message of Hosea is complementary to that of Amos. It is true that God's laws cannot be broken with impunity, but with God there is always room for repentance and a constant invitation to return to his love. In Canaanite worship the Baal (or lord and master) was husband to the land, thus ensuring its fertility. So strong was this influence that by the time of Hosea the people of Israel were regarding the Lord himself as husband of the land. Hosea uses all his passion and poetry to make men see that the Lord is wedded to the people morally and spiritually, and not to the land. He will treat them with justice, kindness and mercy; they must honour their side of the union by faithfulness, love and worship.*

Chapters 4–14 present great difficulties. The Hebrew is sometimes unintelligible, and the messages themselves appear to be muddled and repetitive. No doubt this is partly due to the fact that they were delivered on different occasions and later collected into a

27

*book. But there seems to be some evidence that the confusion is due
to the very great emotional stress under which Hosea is speaking.
Promises and threats often seem confused, and the picture of husband
and wife puzzlingly changes to that of a father and child. We need
to remember that the prophet is "in the thick of it", himself feeling
and suffering with his own people.*

*Where Amos thunders of the wrath which must follow Israel's
breaking of God's laws, Hosea feels the whole tragedy as one of
unfaithfulness and disloyalty in the face of God's unchanging love.*

CHAPTER ONE

1 The word of the Lord which came to Hosea, son of Beeri
while Uzziah, Jotham, Ahaz and Hezekiah were kings of
Judah, and Jeroboam, son of Joash, was the king of Israel.

The Lord's strange command and its parabolic meaning

2 While Hosea was waiting, the word of the Lord came to
him, saying, Go and marry a faithless woman, and have
children from her unfaithfulness, for the land commits
wholesale prostitution in forsaking the Lord.

3 So he went and took Gomer, the daughter of Diblaim,
and she conceived and bore him a son.

4 Then the Lord said to him, Give him the name of Jezreel,
for it will not be long before I punish the house of Jehu for
the blood of Jezreel, and utterly destroy the kingdom of
the house of Israel.

5 For the day shall come when I will break the power
of Israel in the valley of Jezreel.

The Lord withdraws his pity from Israel

6 Gomer conceived again and gave birth to a daughter. The
Lord said to Hosea, Call her by the name of Unloved for I

will no longer have pity on the house of Israel, nor will I forgive them any more.

The divine deliverance of Judah

7 But as for the house of Judah I will have pity on them, and I will deliver them by the Lord their God. It will not be by bow, nor sword, nor by horsemen in battle that I shall deliver them.

Gomer's third child is also a parable

8 When Gomer had weaned Unloved, she conceived and gave
9 birth to a son. And the Lord said, Give him the name of Stranger, for you are strangers to me and I am not your God.

Yet the Prophet foresees eventual triumph

10 Nevertheless the number of the people of Israel shall surely be like the sands of the sea, which can neither be measured nor counted. And in the very place where they were called Strangers to me, they shall be called Sons of the living God.
11 Both the children of Judah and the children of Israel shall be gathered together, and shall appoint for themselves one leader. And they shall rise up from the land, for glorious and terrible shall be the day of Jezreel.

CHAPTER TWO

1 Speak to your brothers and call them now, My People, and call your sisters Beloved!

The Lord speaks to the unfaithful nation

2 Put your mother on trial, plead with her!
(For she is no wife of mine and I am not her husband.)
Tell her to wash the paint from her face,
And the seductions from between her breasts;

3 Or else I will strip her naked,
Bare as the day she was born;
I will make her like a desolate land,
I will let her become like a dried-up desert,
And leave her to die of thirst.

4 I will have no pity either upon her children,
For they are the children of her shame.

5 For their mother has played the harlot,
The one who conceived them has been shameless;
For she said, I will keep following my lovers,
Who give me bread and water,
My wool and my flax, my oil and my wine.

6 Therefore I shall block all her paths with thorns,
I will wall her in so that she cannot find her way out.

7 She will chase after her lovers,
But she will never catch them,
She will search for them,
But she will never find them.
And then she will say,
Let me go back to my first husband,
It was better for me then than it is now!

8 Yet not once has she realised
That I was the one who gave her
The grain, the wine, and the oil;

I was the one who lavished upon her silver and gold,
Which they used in making images of Baal.

The nation must be brought to her senses—

9   Therefore when the corn is ripe I shall take it away,
And when the wine is ready, I will take it back.
And when the wool and flax are ready to clothe her,
I will snatch them away.
10   And I shall expose her for what she is
In the eyes of her lovers,
And no man shall rescue her from my hand.

—by severe punishment

11   For I will put a stop to her pleasures;
Her feasts, her new moons, her sabbaths,
And all her ceremonial feasts.
12   I will blast her vines and her fig trees,
Of which she used to say, This is what I have earned,
These are the gifts which my lovers gave me.
I will turn them into a jungle
And wild beasts shall devour them.
13   And I will see that she pays for the feast-days of the Baals,
When she burned incense in their honour,
And decked herself with that ring of hers and all that
      jewellery,
And pursued her lovers
And forgot me, says the Lord.

The Lord is her true lover

14   See, now, I will be the one who attracts her,
And brings her into a desert place,
And speaks gently to her inmost heart.
15   From there I will give her her vineyards,

31

And turn the valley of Bitterness
Into a pass which is bright with promise.
And there she will respond
As she did in the days of her youth,
As she did at the time when she came
Out of the land of Egypt.

The Lord promises reconciliation and peace

16 And in that day, says the Lord, you shall say to me, My
husband. You shall no longer say to me, My lord and
17 master. For I will wipe her lips clean from the names of her
lords and masters, and they shall never be remembered
again.

18   On that day I will make an agreement between them and
the beasts of the field, the birds of the air and the creeping
things of the ground. And I will break the bow and the
sword and all the tools of war in the land and I will let them
lie down in security.

The Lord and his people will be united

19   I will take you to be my wife for ever.
I will take you to be my wife rightly and justly,
I will take you in kindness and mercy.
20   I will take you to be my wife in faithfulness,
And you shall know the Lord.

Prosperity will come—

21   In that day, says the Lord,
I will respond to the appeal of the heavens.
·And they shall respond to the earth,
22   And the earth shall respond to the grain, the wine and the
oil,
And they will be the answer to Jezreel.

—and complete restoration

23 And I will sow her for myself in the land.
  For I will love Unloved
  And I will say to Stranger,
  You are My People,
  And they will say, You are My God.

CHAPTER THREE

Yet, in the present, the Prophet must again act a parable

1 Then the Lord said to me, Go once more and love this
  woman who is loved by an evil man and is an adulteress—
  just as the Lord loves the people of Israel although they turn
  to other gods and love the raisin-cakes of idolatry.
2 So I bought her for myself for a handful of silver and a
3 sack and a half of barley. Then I said to her, You will live
  quietly with me for many days. There is to be no more
  playing the harlot or giving yourself to another man and I,
  for my part, will leave you alone.

As with Hosea's wife, so with Israel

4 For the children of Israel shall live quietly for many days
  without a king, without a prince, without sacrifice, without
  a sacred stone, without idols or wooden images.
5 Then the time will come when the sons of Israel shall
  return and seek the Lord their God and David their king,
  and in the end they will come in awe to the Lord and his
  goodness.

CHAPTER FOUR

But now evil is rife and the land suffers

1   Now hear what the Lord says, you people of Israel,
    For the Lord has a quarrel with the inhabitants of the
        land!
    There is no honesty nor compassion nor knowledge of
        God,
2   But an outbreak of cursing, murder, stealing and adultery,
    And bloodshed follows bloodshed.
3   This is why the land is withered,
    And everyone who lives in it has lost heart,
    Yes, even the beasts in the field and the birds in the air,
    While the fish have disappeared from the sea.

The fault lies with the spiritual leaders

4   Yet let no one find fault and let no one condemn,
    For my quarrel is with you, you priestling!
5   You have stumbled today,
    And tonight the prophet will stumble with you,
    And I will destroy the one who gave you birth.

The priests are condemned and rejected

6   My people are dying for lack of knowledge,
    And because you have rejected knowledge
    I reject you from being priest to me.
    Because you have forgotten the Law of your God
    I, for my part, will forget your children.
7   For the more they grow in numbers,
    The more they have sinned against me.
    They have changed a glorious calling into a shameful
        trade.

8   They feed on my people's sins
     And lick their lips over the guilt to come.

9   There is nothing to choose between priest and people.
     I will punish them for their ways
     And repay them for their deeds.

10 They may eat but they will not be satisfied,
     They may commit adultery but they will have no
       children,
     Because they have forgotten the Lord.

11 Lust and wine have taken away their senses.

The people are lost and ruined

12 My people! Asking advice from a piece of wood
     And consulting a staff for instructions!
     It is the spirit of lust that has led them astray,
     And they have left their God, to follow the paths of
       unfaithfulness.

13 They make their sacrifices on the mountain-tops
     And their offerings on the hills,
     Beneath oak-trees or poplars or willows
     Because of their pleasant shade.
     And so your daughters become prostitutes
     And your married women commit adultery.

14 I will not punish your daughters for their prostitution
     Nor your married women for their adultery,
     For the leaders themselves go off with prostitutes
     And sacrifice with the harlots of the shrines—
     No wonder the senseless people are brought to ruin!

A warning to Judah not to follow Israel

15 You, Israel, may play the harlot,
     But let not Judah share your guilt.
     Never go to Gilgal, nor climb up to Bethaven,
     Never take the oath, My God!

16   Israel is as obstinate as a stubborn heifer.
How can the Lord feed them now
Like lambs in a broad meadow?

17   Ephraim is wedded to idolatry,
Let him alone.

18   They are a crowd of drunkards given over to lust,
Loving their shameful worship more than my glory.

19   But when the wind whirls them away
They will be ashamed of their altars.

CHAPTER FIVE

The Lord's stern warning

1   Hear this, you priests,
Pay attention, you house of Israel,
Listen, you royal house!
For this judgement is pronounced against you:
Like hunters you have set your snares at Mizpah,
You have spread your nets on the slopes of Tabor,

2   And dug a deep pit at Shittim;
But I am the one who is the hunter
And all of you shall be my prey.

3   I am the one who knows Ephraim,
And Israel cannot hide from me.
For now that you have played the harlot, Ephraim,
Israel is defiled.

Sin means separation from God

4   It is their deeds which block their pathway back to God,
For their spirit is steeped in unfaithfulness
And they know nothing of the Lord.

5   The very arrogance of Israel testifies against him,
Ephraim goes stumbling along in his guilt
And Judah shall stumble also.

36

6 With their flocks and herds, they shall go in search of the
    Lord.
  But they shall not find him.
  For he has withdrawn himself from them.
7 They have been unfaithful to the Lord,
  And borne children who are none of his.
  Any month now may bring ruin to them and their fields.

The Prophet gives solemn warning—

8 Blow the horn in Gibeah
  And the trumpet in Ramah,
  Sound the alarm in Bethaven
  And make Benjamin tremble in fear!
9 Ephraim shall be utterly desolate in the day of punish-
    ment.
  Here among the tribes of Israel I declare what is sure and
    certain.

—disaster follows sin

10 The leaders of Judah have become like common land-
     thieves,
   I will vent my wrath upon them like a flood.
11 Ephraim is in agony and crushed in judgement
   Because his mind was set on following false gods.
12 That is why I am the moth which rots the fabric of
     Ephraim,
   I am the dry-rot which ruins the house of Judah.

The Lord is the only refuge

13 When Ephraim saw how ill he had become,
   And Judah saw how he had been wounded,
   Then Ephraim turned to Assyria
   And sent a message to the great king.

37

But he has no power to cure your sickness,
Nor to heal your wound.

14   For I, myself, am like a lion to Ephraim,
Like a young lion in the house of Judah.
Yes, I will rend and go on my way,
I will carry off my prey and no one can take it from me.

The Lord will hide his face: his people seek him—

15   I will go back once more to my own place,
Until they admit their guilt and seek my face,
And in their misery they will search for me saying,

CHAPTER SIX

1   Come, let us go back to the Lord;
For he has torn us and he will heal us,
He has wounded us and he will bind us up.

2   In a day or two he will revive us,
And on the third day he will set us on our feet
To live beneath his care.

3   Let us know the Lord, let us be determined to know him;
For he will come back to us as surely as the dawn,
As surely as the rains fall in winter,
And as the showers which water the earth in spring.

—but will they ever understand his ways?

4   What can I make of you, Ephraim?
What can I make of you, Judah?
For your love is like a morning cloud,
Like the misty dew which disappears so soon.

5   This is why I have cut them down by the prophets,
And killed them by the words of my mouth,
And my judgement strikes like lightning.

6   It is true love that I have wanted, not sacrifice;
The knowledge of God rather than burnt-offerings.

7   But they, like Adam, have broken their agreement;

38

Again and again they have played me false.

8 Gilead is a city of evil men, stamped with bloody foot-
prints.

9 As bandits lie in wait for their victim,
So a gang of priests murder those who go to Shechem.
Yes, they are criminals indeed!

Continued evil makes forgiveness impossible

10 In the house of Israel I have seen a dreadful thing;
For Ephraim has played the harlot and Israel is defiled.

11 And for you too, Judah, the harvest is inevitable.
When I would bring prosperity back to my people,

CHAPTER SEVEN

1 When I long to make Israel whole,
Then the guilt of Ephraim is exposed
And all the evil of Samaria.
For there is not an honest man among them—
Thieves walk in and out of houses,
And bandits roam the streets.

2 They are a faithless people,
But I shall faithfully record all their evil.
Now they are hemmed in by their own deeds
And they must face me.

Israel's corruption in high places

3 Their evil deeds amuse their king,
And their treacheries entertain their leaders.

4 For they are all adulterers;
Inside they are burning hot as an oven;
The baker has ceased to stoke the fire
Yet the kneaded dough is rising.

5 At the king's festival the leaders made themselves sick,
They were inflamed with wine,
While the king joined hands with the loose and worthless.

39

6   Their hearts burn like an oven with their intriguing,
      Their fury smoulders all night long,
      And in the morning blazes into a flaming fire.

7   They are all as hot as an oven,
      They consume their own rulers—
      King after king has fallen—
      And not one of them called for me.

Israel's disloyalty and folly

8   Israel has lost himself among strangers,
      Ephraim is half-baked—scorched on one side and un-
          cooked on the other!

9   His strength is sapped by foreigners,
      And he does not know it.
      His hair is sprinkled with grey,
      And he does not know it.

10   But now the pride of Israel is plain to him—
      That they have not returned to the Lord their God.
      Yet, despite all this, they do not search for him.

11   And so Ephraim has become a silly dove,
      A witless, foolish creature.
      For they call to Egypt, or they go to Assyria.

12   But as they go I will throw my net over them,
      I will bring them down like birds in the air,
      I will punish them for their wickedness.

It is the Lord whom they have forgotten

13   Woe betide them for straying away from me!
      Death to them for rebelling against me!
      Why should I redeem them
      When they tell lies about me?

14   They have never called for me from their hearts,
      They howl by their altars for food and wine.
      They gash themselves like pagans and rebel against me,

15 Although it was I who trained them to be strong,
While they made evil plans against me.
16 They are converted, but only to false gods;
They are like a bow which never shoots straight.
Because of their arrogant talk,
Which makes them a laughing-stock in the land of Egypt,
Their leaders shall fall by the sword!

CHAPTER EIGHT

Disloyalty means certain destruction

1 Put the trumpet to your lips, sound the alarm!
The eagle swoops down upon the house of the Lord,
Because they broke their covenant with me
And sinned against my law.
2 To me they cry, My God, we know you: we are your
Israel!
3 But Israel has rejected good with loathing—
Now let the enemy hound him down!
4 They have set up kings, but they are not mine;
They have made princes, but I never knew them.
They used their silver and gold to make their idols
Only to see both wasted.
5 Samaria, I reject your calf with loathing!
My anger blazes against them;
6 How long shall they escape scot-free?
This calf, too, was made by a smith in Israel,
It is not God!
No, Samaria's calf shall be smashed to pieces!
7 For they have sown the wind
And their harvest shall be the whirlwind.
Their grain has no stalk
And will yield no flour;
Even if it were to yield,
Strangers would swallow it up!

8   Israel himself has been swallowed up;
    Already he has cheapened himself among the nations.

9   They have gone up to Assyria for help,
    Like a wild ass wandering off on its own,
    And given loving presents for Egypt's aid.

10   If they spend themselves like this among the nations,
    I will soon bring them back again,
    And for a while there will be an end
    To their anointing kings and princes.

The people worship, but with no knowledge of the Lord

11   Ephraim has raised altar after altar,
    And thus has multiplied his sinning.

12   If I were to write out for him
    The ten thousand instructions of my law,
    He would look on them as foreign rules
    And no concern of his!

13   They make sacrifices to me and eat the meat—
    The Lord takes no pleasure in that!
    Now must the Lord remember their guilt
    And punish them for their sins.
    They must go back to another Egypt,

14   For Israel has forgotten his Maker and built palaces,
    While Judah has built fortress after fortress.
    But I will rain fire upon his cities
    And it will devour his palaces and his fortresses.

CHAPTER NINE

Exile is the consequence of unfaithfulness

1   Do not rejoice, Israel,
Do not celebrate like pagans!
For you have played the harlot in forsaking your God.
You have enjoyed a harlot's fee
On every threshing floor.

2   There will be no threshing floor nor wine-vat to feed them
And the promise of the new wine will fail.

3   For they will not remain in the land of the Lord—
Ephraim will go back to a new Egypt
And they will eat unclean food in Assyria!

4   They will pour out no wine before the Lord,
Nor will they prepare sacrifices for him.
Their bread will be the bread which is broken for the
    dead
And all who eat it shall be defiled.
Their food will be for their hunger only—
It cannot be offered in the house of the Lord.

5   What will you do on the day of the festival,
And on the day of the feast of the Lord?

6   For, see, they will go to Assyria—
Egypt to round them up, Memphis to bury them!
Nettles will inherit their treasures of silver
And thorns will occupy their tents.

7a   The days of punishment have come,
The days of recompense are here;
Israel shall know it!

Wicked men hate the truth

7b   The prophet is a fool, is he,
And the man inspired is a man insane?
This shows the depth of your iniquity,

43

The depth of your bitter hatred!

8 The prophet is God's watchman over Ephraim,
Even though there are snares for him everywhere
And he meets fierce enmity in the temple of his God.

9 They have depraved themselves as deeply
As they did in the days of Gibeah,
He will remember their guilt,
And punish them for their sins.

The Lord speaks of Israel's corruption—

10 I discovered Israel
Like grapes in the wilderness.
I looked upon your fathers
As the first fruit on the fig-tree
In its first season.
But when they arrived at Baal-peor
They surrendered themselves utterly to Baal.
They became as abominable
As the thing which they loved.

—and its terrible consequence

11 Ephraim's glory has taken wing like a bird—
No birth, no pregnancy, no conception!

16b Even if they beget children
I will kill the darlings of their womb.

12a Even if they bring up children
I will bereave them till there are no men left!

13 Ephraim's sons are doomed to fall victims,
Ephraim must lead his sons to certain slaughter.

The Prophet's interjection—a bitter prayer

14 Give them O Lord—
What will you give?

44

Give them wombs that miscarry
Give them dry and withered breasts!

The Lord's outraged love

15 All their guilt is centred in Gilgal.
Yes, it was there that I conceived my hatred for them!
Because of their evil doings
I will drive them out of my house.
I will not love them any more
For their leaders are rebels against me.
12b Woe betide them when I turn my eyes away from them!
16a Ephraim is blighted, his root is withered,
Ephraim, the fruitful, bears no fruit.

The Prophet speaks again

17 My God will toss them aside
Because they have not listened to his voice,
And they shall become homeless wanderers
Among the nations!

CHAPTER TEN

Israel's prosperity has meant increased wickedness

1 Israel is a lush and lusty vine
Which bears him luscious grapes!
The more his fruit increased
The more altars did he build;
The more his land prospered
The more he beautified his heathen pillars.
2 They are false at heart
And now they must face their guilt.
The Lord will split their altars
And shatter their pillars.

45

Confusion and disaster must follow

3   Soon they will say, We have no king,
    For if we fail to fear the Lord,
    What can a king do for us?
4   Empty promises, agreements falsely sworn—
    No wonder lawsuits spring up like poisonous weeds
    In the furrows of the field.
5   The citizens of Samaria mourn
    For the fate of the calf of Bethaven.
    Its people shall weep and wail for it,
    Its heathen priests shall writhe for it,
6   Yes, the thing itself shall be carried off to Assyria
    To be offered as a present to the great king.
    Ephraim will be disgraced
    And Israel ashamed of the counsel he followed.
7   As for Samaria, her king shall be tossed aside
    Like a chip on the face of the waters.
8   The high places of Aven, the sin of Israel,
    Shall be utterly destroyed.
    Thorns and thistles shall spring up on their altars
    And they shall say to the mountains, Cover us,
    And to the hills, Fall upon us!

Where Israel first sinned, there shall she be punished

9   Your sins, Israel, all began at Gibeah
     And there you remain defiant still.
     Why should not war overtake them, there in Gibeah?
     In my wrath I will punish them,
10   I will gather nations against them,
     To chastise them for their double sin.

46

Repentance is still possible

11 Ephraim was a trained heifer
Who enjoyed the work of threshing,
And I myself spared her lovely neck.
But now I will put Ephraim under the yoke,
Judah must plough,
Jacob must break up the earth for himself.

12 Sow justice for yourselves
Reap the fruit of love.
Break up the fallow ground
For there is yet time to seek the Lord,
For him to let his justice fall upon you like rain.

Otherwise disaster is certain

13 You have ploughed evil
And you have reaped disaster;
You have had to eat the harvest of your lying.
Because you have trusted in your chariots,
And in the number of your armed men,

14 The din of war will arise among your people
And all your fortresses shall be destroyed.
As Shalman destroyed Beth-arbel
On the day of battle;
When mothers were dashed to pieces
With children in their arms!

15 This will be your fate at my hands, Israel,
Because of the grossness of your evil.
And in the dawn the king of Israel
Will vanish and be seen no more!

CHAPTER ELEVEN

The Lord tells of his love for Israel

1   When Israel was young I came to love him,
And I called him out of Egypt to be my son.

2   But the more I called them
The further they went from me.
They made sacrifices to the Baals
And burnt incense to idols.

3   Yet it was I who taught Ephraim to walk,
Picking them up in my arms.
Yet they never knew that it was I who healed their
    bruises.

4   I led them with gentle encouragement,
Their harness was a harness of love.
I treated them like the man
Who eases the yoke to free the jaws—
Yes, I bent down to them and gave them food.

But Israel will not turn to him

5   They must return to the land of Egypt
Or Assyria must be their king,
Because they have refused to turn to me.

6   The sword shall whirl around in their cities,
Break the defence of their gates,
And destroy them within their fortresses.

7   My people are bent on turning away from me;
The yoke is all they are fit for—
I can love them no more.

The Lord reveals his heart

8   How, oh how, can I give you up, Ephraim!
How, oh how, can I hand you over, Israel!

48

How can I turn you into a Sodom!
How can I treat you like a Gomorrah!
My heart recoils within me,
All my compassion is kindled.
9   I will not give vent to my fierce anger—
I will not destroy Ephraim again.
For I am God and not man,
I am the Holy One in your very midst,
And I have not come to destroy.

The Lord will one day surely restore his people

10   The Lord will roar like a lion,
Yes, he will roar;
And when the Lord roars
His sons will come in haste from the west,
11   Eagerly, like birds out of Egypt
Or doves from the land of Assyria.
And I will bring them back to their homes,
Says the Lord.

But now his people treat him with deceit and distrust

12   Ephraim surrounds me with lies
And the house of Israel with deceit;
Judah walks uncertainly with God,
With the faithful Holy One.

CHAPTER TWELVE

1   All day long Ephraim rounds up the breeze
    And hunts the scorching wind!
    They pile up lies and deceits.
    They make terms with Assyria
    And carry presents of oil into Egypt.

Israel used to live a life of faith

2   The Lord has a quarrel with Israel:
    He will punish Jacob according to his ways
    And repay him according to his deeds.

3a In the womb Jacob took his brother's place.

12 Jacob fled to the land of Aram,
    And there Israel worked as a servant to gain a wife
    And for a wife he herded sheep.

3b With the strength of a man he strove with God—

4   Yes, he struggled with the angel and he won!
    He wept and begged for mercy,
    He met God at Bethel
    And there God spoke to him:

5   (The Lord is the God of hosts
    The Lord is his name)

6   By the help of your God, return to him,
    Hold fast to kindness and justice,
    And put your trust continually in your God!

But material prosperity has ruined him

7   Swindler! He loves to cheat
    With false balances in his hand.

8   And does Ephraim say, Yes, but I have grown rich,
    I have made myself wealthy?
    All his gains can never outweigh

50

The guilt that he has amassed.

9 I am the Lord your God since the days of Egypt,
I will make you live in tents again,
As in the appointed festivals of old.

The Lord uses prophets for his purpose

10 It was I who spoke through the prophets,
It was I who gave vision after vision,
And through the prophets gave you parables.

11 If there is evil in Gilgal
They shall surely be destroyed.
If they sacrifice oxen there,
Their altars shall become like heaps of stones
In the furrows of the field.

13 It was by a prophet that the Lord
Brought Israel up from Egypt,
And by a prophet was he kept safe.

14 Ephraim has given bitter provocation,
And so the Lord will leave him alone with his guilt
And fling his reproaches back at him.

CHAPTER THIRTEEN

Idolatry means indignity and disaster

1 Whenever Ephraim spoke, men trembled;
He was a prince in Israel!
But the worship of Baal made him guilty
And he died.

2 And still they continue in their sinning,
Casting for themselves idols in silver,
Made to their own design;
Just the work of clever fingers,
Yet they call them gods and worship them,
With men giving kisses to calves!

3   Therefore they will vanish like the morning cloud,
     Like the misty dew which disappears so soon;
     Like chaff that swirls up from the threshing-floor
     Or the smoke out of the window.

The Lord, unrecognised, has been their constant deliverer

4   I am the Lord your God
     Who brought you up out of the land of Egypt;
     You have known no God but me,
     And I am your only saviour.
5   It was I who knew you in the desert,
     In the land where there was no water.
6   But when they fed they stuffed themselves,
     They were fed to the full, their hearts grew proud
     And they forgot me.

But now the Lord will turn and rend them

7   So I shall be a lion to them,
     I shall lurk like a leopard in their path,
8   I shall fall upon them like a bear robbed of her cubs
     And tear their breast wide open;
     I shall crunch them like a lion,
     And tear them like a wild beast.
9   I will destroy you, Israel;
     Who can help you?
10   Where is your king now?
     Who can save you?
     Where are all your princes to defend you—
     Those of whom you said,
     Give me kings and princes?
11   Yes, I give you kings in my anger
     And remove them in my fury!
12   Ephraim's guilt is carefully treasured,
     His sin is safely stored.

13   The pangs of childbirth are here,
But he is a foolish child
And will not come out of the womb
When the moment of birth is here.

The Lord plans utter destruction

14   Shall I save them from the power of Sheol,
Shall I redeem them from death?
Death, bring out your plagues!
Sheol, bring out your power to destroy!
I have no mind for compassion.

15   Though he may flourish like reeds in the water
There shall come a wind from the east,
The wind of the Lord,
Blowing up from the desert
Till his fountains are dried up
And his springs are parched.
It shall strip his treasury
Of every precious thing.

16   Samaria must suffer for her guilt
Because she rebelled against her God.
They shall fall by the sword,
Their children shall be dashed to pieces
And their pregnant women ripped open.

CHAPTER FOURTEEN
Repentance is still possible

1   But come home, Israel, come home to the Lord your God!
    For it is your sins which have been your downfall.
2   Take words of repentance with you as you return to the
        Lord;
    Say to him,
    Clear us from all our evil,
    Receive us in mercy,
    And we will repay with our praise and thanksgiving!
3   Assyria can never save us
    And we will ride no more upon Egypt's horses.
    No more will we say, My God
    To our own handiwork,
    For with you the orphan finds pity.

And the Lord will forgive and restore

4   I will heal their unfaithfulness,
    I will love them with all my heart
    Now that my anger has turned away from them.
5   I will fall like dew upon Israel;
    He shall bloom like a lily,
    He shall strike roots like the trees of Lebanon;
6   His shoots shall spring up,
    His beauty will be like the olive-tree
    And his scent like the scent of Lebanon.

The Prophet sees their return

7   They shall come back and live beneath his shadow,
    They shall flourish like a well-watered garden,
    They shall blossom like a vine,
    And their fragrance shall be like the wine of Lebanon.

The Lord himself answers the nation

8 Ephraim asks, What more have I to do with idols?
It is I who have answered him, and I will care for him.
I am ever-green like the cypress
And from me comes all your fruitfulness.

The issues are plain for any who would understand

9 Let the wise man understand these things,
Let the thoughtful man know them.
For the ways of the Lord are fair and straight:
Good men shall flourish in them
But sinners shall stumble and fall.

The First Book of Isaiah

The First Book of Isaiah

THE PROPHET. *The call of Isaiah (which he describes in Chapter 6) came to him in the year 740 B.C. At the time he was already married and had a young son whom he had named, characteristically, The Return-of-the-Remnant. He was a man of Jerusalem, who knew the city, its king and its leaders. His ministry continued there for some twenty-three years. He also had a fair and shrewd knowledge of the great powers which almost surrounded his own country. He was listened to with respect by the king himself as well as by the leaders of the people. Because of his knowledge of the political scene Isaiah was able to communicate the urgency of the situation in terms which would be understood.*

This prophet, unlike the others, was a townsman, a courtier and an aristocrat. His writing is more naturally poetic in language and imagery, and he can see far more clearly than the others that the Lord is the God of all nations. He does not blurt out the truth for the mere sake of being outspoken. Devastating as many of his messages are, they rarely lack (when the text is clear) a certain polish and a potent high poetry.

He was plainly a man of great personal courage, and as the years passed his reputation grew. He did not hesitate to attack the rich and powerful for their evil and selfish ways. Once, at least, he reinforced the urgency of his message by living barefoot and half-clad for three years (Chapter 20). He was still alive in 701, but there is no reliable record of his death.

THE THEME. *The basic theme of Isaiah's teaching is that it is God and not man, who determines history, whatever appearances may suggest. Therefore true peace and true prosperity can only be achieved by quietly carrying out the will of the Lord. Clever political moves and alliances may appear advantageous, but they are useless and indeed evil if they lead the nation away from its trust in God. Isaiah sees the nation as estranged from the Lord, not only by its lack of faith in him, but by its pre-occupation with material prosperity and its utter indifference to the gravest social evils. Like the other true prophets of the period he saw injustice towards men as a flagrant offence against God and he denounced it accordingly.*

The prophecies collected in this book seem to mix warnings and promises, somewhat to our confusion. The reason for this is simply that God is offering man a choice. If the nation turns whole-heartedly to the Lord, security in the best, spiritual, sense is assured, even if there are considerable material losses. But if the nation per-sists in putting confidence in foreign alliances and continues to be greedy and corrupt, then the most terrible disasters are bound to follow. Nevertheless, even if the worst happens, Isaiah's con-fidence in God is unshaken. Even after defeat and exile there will be the Remnant to return, chastened and purified, to their own land.

CHAPTER ONE

1 This is what Isaiah, the son of Amoz, saw to be true about Judah and Jerusalem during the reigns of Uzziah, Jotham, Ahaz, and Hezekiah, kings of Judah.

Israel's unfaithfulness has meant her destruction

2 Let the heavens hear
And let the earth listen.
For the Lord has spoken:
I have nourished children
And brought them up,
But they have rebelled against me;

3 The ox knows its owner,
And the ass its master's manger,
But Israel does not care,
My people give me no thought.

4   You are a nation rotten to the core!
    A people bowed down with guilt,
    A generation of evil-doers,
    Sons who cheat and lie!
    They have forsaken the Lord,
    They have despised the Holy One of Israel,
    And made themselves utter strangers to him.

Can she not see her condition?

5   Why must you invite further punishment?
    Why continue in your rebellion?
    Your whole head is sick,
    And your whole heart diseased.
6   From the sole of your feet to the top of your head
    No single part is sound.
    Nothing but bruises and sores
    And still bleeding wounds,
    Which are neither squeezed out nor bandaged,
    Nor softened with oil.
7   Your land is a desert,
    Your cities are burned down.
    Before your eyes strangers devour the fields you tilled.
8   The daughter of Zion is left
    Like a hut in a vineyard,
    Like a shelter in a cucumber field,
    Like a lonely watch-tower.
9   If the Lord of hosts
    Had not allowed some of us to escape,
    We should have been like Sodom
    We should become like Gomorrah.

The Lord requires righteousness—not ritual

10 Hear the word of the Lord,
    You rulers of Sodom!

    Listen to the instruction of our God
    You people of Gomorrah!

11   What use to me are your innumerable sacrifices?
    I am sick of the burnt rams offered to me
    And of the grease of fattened beasts.
    I get no pleasure from the blood of bulls,
    Nor of lambs nor of he-goats!
    Who requires such things from you

12   When you come into my presence?
    I will not have you trampling my courts,

13   Let us have no more of these gifts!
    The smoke of your sacrifices is detestable to me,
    I cannot bear your calls to prayer at Sabbath or new moon,

14   With my soul I hate your fasts and festivals.
    They have become a burden to me
    And I am weary of carrying it.

15   When you spread out your hands in prayer
    I will turn my face away from you;
    Yes, even though you make many prayers,
    I shall not listen.
    Your hands are dripping with blood,

16   Cleanse yourselves; make yourselves pure!
    Take the evil of your doings
    Out of my sight!
    Cease to do wrong,

17   Learn to do good,
    Seek justice,
    Restrain violence,
    Defend the right of the orphan,
    Champion the cause of the widow.

The Lord's invitation—and warning

18   Come, now, and let us settle the matter, says the Lord,
    Though your sins are like scarlet
    They shall be as white as snow;

Though they are red like crimson
They shall become like wool.

19 If you are willing and obedient, you shall live on the fat
of the land,

20 But if you refuse and rebel then husks will be your food.

The present corruption of Jerusalem

21 See what a slut the city has become—
She who was once so true,
She who was just in all her ways!
Once a home of righteousness, now a haunt of murderers.

22 Your silver has become dross,
Your wine spoiled with water.

23 Your rulers obey no rules
And are hand in glove with thieves.
Every one loves a bribe
And is greedy for his profit.
They never defend the right of the orphan
And the widow's cause never comes up before them!

The Lord promises retribution, and eventual restoration

24 Therefore, says the Lord,
The Lord of hosts, the Mighty One of Israel:
Ah, now I will enjoy my revenge upon my foes,
I will avenge myself on my enemies.

25 I will turn my hand against you;
I will burn out all your dross
And remove all your alloy.

26 I will give you judges as at first
And counsellors as at the beginning;
And after that you will be called City of Justice,
The Faithful City.

27 Justice will be the redemption of Zion
And of all those in her who repent.

28 But rebels and sinners shall be destroyed together
And those who forsake the Lord shall be consumed.

29 For you shall be ashamed of the sacred trees which once
delighted you
And blush for the gardens that once you chose.

30 For you yourselves will become like a tree with withered
leaves
And like a garden without water.

31 The strong shall become like kindling
And the idols they have made like a spark,
And both shall burn together
In a blaze that none can quench.

CHAPTER TWO

Jerusalem as she might be

1 And this is what Isaiah, the son of Amoz, saw to be true
about Judah and Jerusalem:

2 In the last days it will come to pass
That the mountain of the Lord
Shall tower above the peaks,
Lifted high above the hills,
And all the nations shall swarm to it!

3 Many peoples will arrive and say,
Come, let us go up to the mountain of the Lord,
And to the house of the God of Jacob.
He will give us knowledge of his ways,
And we will follow in his paths.
For the Law goes forth from Zion,
And the Word of the Lord from Jerusalem.

4 And he will judge between the nations,
And make decision between the peoples.
Then they shall hammer their swords into plough-
shares,

And their spears into pruning-hooks.
Nation shall lift no sword against nation,
And never again will they learn to make war.

5 Come now, house of Jacob, let us walk in the light of the
Lord.

Riches and corruption will be judged by the Lord

6 The Lord has abandoned his people, the house of Jacob.
Their land is full of soothsayers
And of fortune-tellers like the Philistines.
His people make bargains with the children of foreigners;
7 Their land is filled with silver and gold
And their treasure is past counting.
Their land teems with horses
And their chariots are innumerable.
8 Their land has become full of idols
And they bow down to the work of their hands,
To things which their fingers have fashioned,
9 And I will not forgive them!

The terror of the day of the Lord

10 Get into caves in the rocks
Hide in holes in the ground
Away from the terror of the Lord,
Away from the glory of his majesty!
11 So the pride of man is humbled
And man's arrogance brought low—
The Lord alone shall be exalted in that day.

12 For the Lord of hosts has a day of reckoning
Against all that is proud and haughty,
Against all that is high and lofty—
13 Against all cedars of Lebanon,
Against all oaks of Bashan,

14   Against all high mountains,
     Against all lofty hills,
15   Against every high tower,
     Against every fortified wall,
16   Against every vessel of Tarshish,
     Against every stately ship.
17   And the arrogance of men shall be brought low
     And the pride of men be humbled.
     The Lord alone will be exalted in that day,
18   And every single idol shall disappear.

19   Then men shall get into caves in the rocks
     And into holes in the ground,
     Away from the terror of the Lord,
     Away from the glory of his majesty,
     When he rises to strike the earth with terror!
20   In that day men will fling to the moles and bats
     Their gold and silver idols,
     Which they made for themselves to worship.
21   And they will get into deep fissures in the rock,
     Into clefts in the cliffs,
     Away from the terror of the Lord,
     Away from the glory of his majesty,
     When he rises to strike the earth with terror!

What, after all, is man?

22   Put no further trust in man
     Who only lives while he breathes,
     For of what account is he?

CHAPTER THREE

Ruin and misgovernment everywhere

1 See now, here is the Lord, the Lord of hosts removing every staff and stay from Jerusalem and Judah—bread, the staff of
2 life, and water its support; the strong man and the warrior; the judge and the prophet, the seer and the elder; the captain
3 of fifty and the man of reputation; the skilled magician and the expert in charms.

4   And I will make mischievous boys their leaders
    And let them be led by the nose.

5   The people will oppress each other, man exploiting man,
    Yes, every man his neighbour.
    The young shall behave rudely towards the old
    And the inferior towards those of high repute.

6   Then a man shall take hold of his fellow,
    (Whose family owns a robe of office),
    And say, You have a robe, you shall be our ruler,
    You shall be king of this pile of rubble!

7   In that day he will protest plainly,
    I cannot repair the ruin,
    My family has no bread
    And there is no robe of office;
    You cannot make me ruler of the people.

8   For Jerusalem has stumbled
    And Judah has fallen;
    Their words and their deeds defy the Lord,
    Insulting his glorious presence.

9   Their besotted folly condemns them;
    They flaunt their sin like Sodom
    And make no attempt to hide it.
    Alas for them, for they brought evil upon themselves.

10   Happy is the good man, it shall be well for him,
    For he shall eat the fruit of his deeds.

11   But alas for the wicked, it shall go ill for him,
      For what he has done shall be his own undoing!
12   My people are cruelly oppressed—by children,
      And their ways are ruled by women.
      Your leaders are misleading you, my people,
      They are confusing the path in which you should go!

But the Lord condemns the rulers and leaders

13   The Lord enters the court,
      The Lord stands to judge his people;
14   And the Lord calls to account the elders and leaders of the
         people:
      It is you who have stripped my vineyard bare,
      Your houses hoard what you have plundered from the
        poor!
15   What do you mean by crushing my people,
      By grinding the faces of the poor?
      This is what the Lord of hosts says.

The doom of Jerusalem's fine ladies

16   The Lord has also said:
      Because the daughters of Zion are high and mighty,
      Walking with their noses in the air,
      Flirting with their eyes,
      Mincing along with jingling anklets,
17   The Lord shall strike their scalps with scabs
      And uncover what they keep hidden.

18 In that day the Lord will take away the luxury of anklets,
19 headbands and moon-charms, ear-rings, bracelets and
20 scarves, head-dresses, armlets and sashes, scent-bottles, magic
21 charms, signet rings and nose-rings, party dresses, cloaks,
22 stoles and handbags, revealing clothes, linen garments, splen-
23 did turbans and outdoor veils.

24 Instead of perfume there will be the stench of disease,
Instead of a girdle there will be a length of rope,
Instead of well-groomed hair a bald head,
Instead of a fine dress a bit of sackcloth,
Branding instead of beauty-treatment!

25 Your men shall die by the sword
And your strong men in battle;

26 The city-gates shall mourn and wail,
And the city sit upon the ground, desolate and forlorn.

CHAPTER FOUR

1 And seven women shall take hold of one man in that day,
saying, We will earn our own living and wear our own
clothes; only let us be called by your name and saved from
disgrace!

After judgement the Lord promises prosperity and security

2 But the day will come when the green growth of the
Lord shall be gloriously beautiful,
And the fruit of the land shall be the pride and joy of
Israel's survivors.

4 When the Lord has washed away the filth from Zion's
daughters,
And rinsed Jerusalem clean from the bloodstains in her
midst
With the spirit of judgement
And the spirit of purging fire,

3 Then those who are left in Zion
Those who remain in Jerusalem
Shall be called holy—
All those in Jerusalem whose names are written in the
Book of Life.

5   And over the whole of Mount Zion the Lord will form a
        cloud by day
     And over her assemblies a canopy of light—
     A flaming fire in the darkness of the night.
6   It will be shade by day from the scorching heat
     And a safe refuge from storm and rain.

CHAPTER FIVE

A parable in song and its obvious meaning

1   Now let me sing about my loved one
     A song about his vineyard
     My loved one had a vineyard
     On a sunny fertile hill.
2   He dug up the ground and cleared it of stones,
     And he planted it with the finest vines.
     He built a watch-tower in the middle of it
     And he hewed out a vat for pressing out the wine.
     He expected it to produce grapes
     But all it produced were wild grapes.
3   Now, you who live in Jerusalem
     And you men of Judah,
     I ask you to judge between me and my vineyard.
4   What else could I have done for my vineyard,
     What did I fail to do?
     Why, when I expected it to produce grapes,
     Did it produce wild grapes?

5   And now let me tell you
     What I shall do to my vineyard.
     I shall tear down its hedge so that it is eaten up,
     I will break down its wall so that it is trampled flat.
6   I will make it a waste land,
     It shall be neither hoed nor weeded
     And briars and thorns will spring up in it.

I will even command the clouds
To drop no rain upon it.

7   For the vineyard of the Lord of hosts
Is the house of Israel,
And the men of Judah the planting in which he delighted.
He looked for justice, and, see, there is anarchy,
He looked for righteousness, and, listen, a cry from the
    oppressed!

Greed will lead to famine

8   Woe to those who join house to house,
Who add field to field
Until there is no room for any but themselves
In all the land!
9   The Lord of hosts has sworn, and I heard him,
Many houses shall be deserted,
Fine stately houses with no one to live in them!
10   Ten acres of vineyard will produce only a few gallons,
And the harvest of grain will be but a tenth of the seed
    that is sown.

Self-indulgence means certain disaster

11   Woe to those who get up early in the morning
To begin their drinking;
Who sit far into the night
Inflamed by wine!
12   At their feasting they have harps and lutes, drums and
    flutes
As well as wine.
But they are blind to the purpose of the Lord
Nor do they see what he is doing.
13   Therefore my people have gone into exile
With no knowledge of the Lord;

Their leaders are famished with hunger
And the people parched with thirst.

14   Therefore the land of the dead has grown even more
       hungry
And its jaws gape wide;
Down go the nobility of Jerusalem
And all her people
With their noise and shouts of joy!

15   Man is humbled; men are brought low,
The eyes of the proud are downcast,

16   But the Lord of hosts is exalted by his justice.
The Holy God has shown himself holy in righteousness,

17   While lambs graze in their pasture
And kids feed among the ruins.

Men who provoke the Lord's anger

18   Woe to those who pull guilt down upon themselves with
      cords of wickedness
And drag their sin along as if by a cart-rope!

19   Men who say, Let him make haste,
Let him hurry so that we may see what he is doing!
Let the purpose of the Holy One of Israel come closer,
Let it be fulfilled, so that we may know what it is!

20   Woe to those who call evil good, and good evil;
Who make out light to be darkness, and darkness light,
Sweet to be bitter, and bitter sweet!

21   Woe to those who think themselves wise
And fancy themselves so shrewd!

22   Woe to those who are heroes—at drinking,
Who are mighty men—at mixing drinks!

23   Men who release the guilty for a bribe
And cheat the innocent of his right to go free.

24   Therefore as fire licks up the stubble
And dry grass falls to ashes in the flame,
So shall their roots be seen to be rotten

And their opening blossoms seen to be dust!
For they have spurned the commands of the Lord of hosts
And despised the word of the Holy One of Israel.
25   This is why the anger of the Lord blazed against his people,
And he stretched out his hand against them,
Striking them till the mountains trembled
And their corpses lay like refuse in the streets!
And yet his anger is not satisfied,
And his arm is still upraised to strike.

The Lord will use another nation for his purpose

26   Then he will signal for a nation afar off
And whistle for it from the other end of the earth.
And suddenly it comes, swiftly, quickly,
27   None fainting, none stumbling,
None slumbering nor sleeping;
Not a belt is loose,
Not a shoe-string broken,
28   Arrows all sharp,
Bows all bent,
Horses' hoofs as hard as flint,
Wheels like whirlwinds,
29   With the roar of a lioness
And the roar of young lions
It will seize its victim with a snarl
And carry it off, with none to rescue!
30   His roaring on that day
Will be like the roaring of the sea.
The land shows nothing but darkness and misery,
The light blotted out by clouds of dust.

CHAPTER SIX

The Prophet's vision and call

1 In the year of King Uzziah's death, I saw the Lord seated high on a lofty throne, while the train of his robes flowed
2 over the temple floor. Seraphs hovered around him, each with six wings—two to cover their faces, two to cover their
3 feet and two to keep them in the air. They kept calling to each other, crying:

Holy, holy, holy is the Lord of hosts
The whole earth is full of his glory.

4 The doorway shook to its foundations at the sound of their voices, and smoke began to fill the temple.
5 Then I said, Alas for me—for I am finished! I am a foul-mouthed man and I live among a foul-mouthed people. For with my own eyes I have seen the King, the Lord of hosts.
6 Then one of the seraphs flew towards me carrying a red-hot coal which he had taken with tongs from the altar. With
7 this he touched my mouth saying, See, now your guilt shall go and your sin be forgiven!
8 Then I heard the voice of the Lord, saying:

Whom shall I send?
Who will go for us?

9 And I said, Here am I: send me. Then he said, Go, and say to this people:

Listen and listen but never understand the meaning!
Look and look but never see the point!
10 Make this people thick in the head,
Seal up their ears, stick down their eyelids,
Or else their eyes will see, their ears will hear,
Their minds will understand
And they will be restored to health again!

11 Then I said, How long, Lord? And he said:

> Until they are utterly ruined—
> Their cities deserted,
> Their houses empty,
> And their land left desolate;

12 Until the Lord banishes men to far-off places
> And most of the land is a desert.

13 Yet if even a tenth of them remain,
> Even these must be burnt out
> Like the felled stump of an oak or pine.
> And yet this stump is a holy seed.

CHAPTER SEVEN

King Ahaz is alarmed

1 During the time that Ahaz (son of Jotham, son of Uzziah) was king of Judah, Rezin, king of Syria with Pekah (son of Remaliah) king of Israel, came up to attack Jerusalem but 2 failed in their attempt. When the king's court was told, Syria has occupied Ephraim, the heart of Ahaz and of his people quivered as the trees in the forest tremble before the wind.

But the Prophet is told there is no need to fear

3 But the Lord said to Isaiah, Go out with your son Shear-jashub (Return-of-the-Remnant) and meet Ahaz at the end of the aqueduct from the upper pool, on the road to the 4 Fuller's Field. Tell him, Keep calm and do not be fearful. Never be afraid of the smouldering stumps of those two fire-brands, Rezin of Syria and Remaliah's son, with all their blazing fury.

The threat will come to nothing

5 Syria with Ephraim and Remaliah's son has planned mis-
6 chief against you, saying, Let us invade Judah, and harass her.
Let us break in and seize the city for ourselves and set up
7 the son of Tabeel upon her throne. But the Lord God has
declared:

> This plan shall not succeed,
> It shall never come to pass.

8a   Damascus is no more than the capital of Syria,
     And Rezin only the king of Damascus.

9   Samaria is no more than the capital of Ephraim,
     And Remaliah's son is only the king of Samaria.
     Without firm faith there is no firm stand.

8b (Sixty-five years from now Ephraim shall be so shattered
that it will cease to be a people)

The Lord offers Ahaz a sign

10, 11 The Lord spoke again to Ahaz: Ask for a Sign from the
Lord your God, ask for it in the depth of the underworld or
in the heights of heaven.
12   But Ahaz said, I will not ask, and I will not put the Lord to
13 any test. Then I said, Listen, you house of David! Are you
not satisfied with trying the patience of men? Must you try
the patience of my God also?
14   Because you will not ask, the Lord himself will give you a
Sign. See, a maiden shall conceive and give birth to a son,
and shall call him Immanuel, which means, God is with us.
15 He will eat curds and honey before he is old enough to know
16 good food from bad. Indeed before the boy knows how to
refuse the bad and choose the good, the land, whose two
17 kings so terrify you, will be deserted. The Lord shall bring
upon you, your people and your father's house such a time
as has never been since Ephraim broke with Judah.

The Lord will bring desolation to the faithless land

18 For in that day the Lord shall whistle up the flies and the bees.
19 And they will come in swarms and settle in steep ravines, in
clefts in the rocks, on all the thorn bushes and over all the
20 pastures. In that day the Lord will use a razor, hired from the
banks of the Euphrates, the king of Assyria! It will shave off
every hair from head to foot and even sweep off your beard.
21   In that day a man will keep only a young cow and two
22 sheep. And because there will be plenty of milk from them
his food must be curds; for any survivor in the land will have
23 curds and honey. In that day every place which once bore a
thousand vines worth a thousand silver shekels, will be a
24 mass of thorns and briars. Men will come there with bows
25 and arrows, for all the land will be briars and thorns. And as
for the slopes which used to be worked with the hoe, you
will not go there for fear of the thorns and briars. They will
be no more than cattle-tracks and sheep-runs.

CHAPTER EIGHT

The Lord's strange command

1 And then the Lord said to me, Write on some large surface
in plain letters, This belongs to *Quick-pickings-Easy-prey*
2 (Maher-shalal-hash-baz). Have it witnessed for me by two
reliable witnesses, Uriah the priest and Zechariah the son of
3 Jeberechiah. Then I, the prophet, went in to the prophetess.
And when she had conceived and borne a son the Lord said
to me, Now call him *Quick-pickings-Easy-prey*, for before
4 the boy knows how to say Dad, or Mum, the wealth of
Damascus and the spoil of Samaria shall be carried off to the
king of Assyria.

The Lord tells the Prophet of disaster, and confidence

5 But the Lord had not finished and he spoke to me again:

6   Because this people have rejected
        The gently-flowing streams of Shiloah,
        And take a fearful pride in Rezin and Remaliah's son,

7   Now the Lord lets loose upon them
        The strong full flood of the River—
        The king of Assyria in all his glory—
        Overflowing all its channels
        And pouring over all its banks;

8a   And it will sweep on into Judah
        In overflowing torrents,
        Flooding it up to the neck.

Judah's safety in the Lord

8b   But the outstretched wings of the Lord
        Shall cover the land from side to side,
        For God is with us!

9   Consider this, you nations,
        And lose your nerve!
        Listen to this, all you distant countries,
        Prepare for war and lose your nerve.
        Yes, prepare for war and lose your nerve.

10   Plan your plans and they will fail.
        Scheme your schemes and they will come to nothing,
        For God is with us!

The Lord speaks personally to the Prophet

11 This is what the Lord said to me, as I felt the strength of
his hand upon me, as he warned me not to give in to the ways
12 of this people: Pay no attention to the rumours of this
people, and do not be afraid of what they fear nor be in dread

13 of it. It is the Lord of hosts whom you should honour, it is he
14 whom you should fear and he whom you should dread. For
he will indeed become a sanctuary, but he will be a stone to
trip over, a rock over which both houses of Israel shall
stumble. He will be a trap and a snare to the people who live
15 in Jerusalem. Many shall stumble, they shall fall and be
broken. They shall be trapped and caught.

The Prophet seals up his message for the future

16 So I tie up my message and seal the teaching in the presence
17 of my disciples. Then I will wait for the Lord, who is hiding
his face from the house of Jacob, and I will rest my hope in
18 him. See, I and the children whom the Lord has given me
are living signs and omens in Israel from the Lord of hosts
who lives on Mount Zion.

There is no hope or truth, except in the Lord

19 Then when they say to you, Consult the mediums and the
spirits who squeak and gibber, then ask them, Should not a
people consult their God? Why should they call on the dead
20 on behalf of the living? Consult the message and the teaching, for unless they speak according to these, their light is
21 but a false dawn. They will wander through the land, miser-
able and hungry. Hunger will drive them to fury and they
will curse their king and their God. They will look up to
22 heaven and they will look round upon the earth only to see
darkness and distress, misery and gloom—darkness that no
light can pierce.

CHAPTER NINE

1 But there shall be no gloom for her who was once in misery. There was a time when he brought contempt upon the land of Zebulun and the land of Naphtali, but there will come a time when he will bring glory upon the road to the sea, the land beyond Jordan, the Galilee of the nations.

The Prophet foresees the glorious future

2 The people who moved in darkness
Have seen a shining light;
Upon those who lived in the land of the shadow of death
The light has shone!

3 You have made them exuberant with rejoicing
And filled their hearts with joy.
They rejoice before you as harvesters rejoice,
As men who share the spoils of battle.

4 For the yoke which bore him down,
The bar which bowed his shoulder,
The whip which drove him on,
You have smashed to pieces
As in the day of victory over Midian.

5 For the trampling boot of battle
And the garment stained with blood
Shall be burned as fuel in the fire.

6 For to us a child will be born,
To us a son will be given;
And government rests upon his shoulders,
And his name shall be:
Wonderful Counsellor,
Mighty God,
Everlasting Father,
Prince of Peace.

7 His power shall spread unceasingly

And his peace shall not be broken.
He will reign upon the throne of David and over all his
    kingdom,
To establish it and make it firm
With justice and in righteousness,
From this time onwards and for evermore.
The jealous care of the Lord of hosts
Shall bring all this to pass.

The doom of Ephraim

8 The Lord has sent a word against Jacob
    And it will fall upon Israel;
9 And all the people shall know its meaning,
    Ephraim and the inhabitants of Samaria.
    For in their arrogance and impudence they say,
10 Bricks have fallen
    But we will rebuild with dressed stone;
    Sycamore woodwork has been cut down
    But we will replace it with cedar.
11 This is why the Lord prospers their enemies against them,
    And spurs on their adversaries.
12 On the east, Assyrians and on the west, Philistines
    Devour Israel with ravening jaws.
    Yet his anger is not satisfied
    And his arm is still upraised to strike;
13 For the people did not turn to him who struck them,
    Nor seek the Lord of hosts;
14 So the Lord cut off Israel's head and tail,
    Palm-branch and rush in a single day—
15 The elders and the men of honour are the head,
    And the prophet with false messages is the tail.
16 The leaders of this people misled them,
    And those who followed were lost.
17 Therefore the Lord will take no pleasure in their young
    men,

And show no pity for their orphans and widows.
For every one of them is godless and wicked,
Blasphemy is on every lip.
Yet his anger is not satisfied
And his arm is still upraised to strike.

The final horror—civil war

18 For wickedness has burnt like a fire,
Eating up thorns and briars,
Firing the thickets in the forest
Till they twist upwards in a rolling column of smoke.
19 It is the anger of the Lord of hosts which burnt the
land,
And the people preyed upon each other.
20 They sliced on the right hand, and were still hungry,
They ate on the left hand, and were not satisfied.
None will have pity for his brother,
But each will devour his neighbour's flesh—
21 Manasseh tearing at Ephraim, and Ephraim at Manasseh,
And both together tearing at Judah.
Yet his anger is not satisfied
And his arm is still upraised to strike.
1 And woe to those who make iniquitous decrees
And write inhuman orders,
2 So that they rob the needy of their rights
And cheat the poor of their rightful due;
So that widows become their victims
And orphans their easy prey.
3 What will you do then, in the day of judgement,
When the storm from afar breaks upon you?
To whom will you run for help,
And where will you leave your plunder?
4 How will you avoid cowering among the prisoners,
Or falling under the corpses of the slain?

Yet his anger is not satisfied
And his arm is still upraised to strike.

CHAPTER TEN

The arrogance of Assyria

5 And now for Assyria, the whip of my anger
 And the lash of my indignation!
6 I send him against a faithless nation,
 I command him to attack the people who have angered
 me,
 To rob them of their treasure and seize their wealth,
 To trample them down like mud in the streets.
7 But this is not how he thinks,
 And this is not his plan.
 His intention is to destroy;
 To exterminate many nations.
8 He says, Are not my captains as good as kings?
9 What difference is there between Calno and Carchemish,
 Between Hamath and Arpad?
 What difference is there between Samaria and Damascus?
10 Since my own hand has seized idol-loving kingdoms,
 Whose graven images were bigger than those of Jeru-
 salem and Samaria,
11 Shall I not treat Jerusalem and her idols as I have treated
 Samaria and her images?

The Lord will punish Assyria's pride

12 When the Lord has completed his work on mount Zion and
 on Jerusalem, he will punish the impudent boasting of the
13 king of Assyria for his arrogant pride. For he says:

 By the strength of my own hand have I done this,
 And by my clever plans—for I am a man of understanding.

I have moved the frontiers of nations,
I have robbed them of their treasures,
I have toppled their kings into the dust!

14 My hand has reached out, as if into a nest,
To grasp the wealth of the nations.
Like a man collecting eggs
I have ransacked the whole earth;
And no one fluttered a wing at me,
And none dared open his beak in protest!

Such pride is intolerable

15 Is the axe to set itself up against him who wields it?
Is the saw to think itself greater than he who uses it?
It would be like a stick swinging the man who lifts it,
Or a wooden staff brandishing a man, who is no thing of
wood!

16 Therefore the Lord, the Lord of hosts,
Shall send a wasting sickness into his flourishing body,
Beneath his glory a fire will be kindled
Which burns like a flame,

18b Consuming soul and body,
Till he wastes away like a man diseased.

17 The light of Israel shall become a fire
And his Holy One a burning flame.
In one day it shall burn up his thorns and briars,

18a His splendid woods and fruitful fields,

19 Till any trees left will be so few
That any child could count them.

The Prophet sees the distant future

20 In that day the survivors of Israel and those who are left of
the house of Jacob will no longer lean upon him that struck
them, but will lean in faithful trust upon the Lord, the Holy

84

21 One of Israel. All who are left, the survivors of Jacob, will
22 return to the mighty God. For though the people of Israel
are like the sand of the sea, only a band of survivors will
return. Destruction has been determined, to prove beyond
23 doubt the righteous purpose of the Lord. For the Lord, the
Lord of hosts, will complete the destruction he has determined, for all the world to see.

The Lord reassures his people in the present crisis

24 Therefore the Lord, the Lord of hosts, says this: My people,
who live in Zion, never be afraid of the Assyrians, though
they strike you with clubs and whip you as the Egyptians did
25 long ago. For within a little while my anger will be spent,
26 and my wrath shall be turned to destroy them. The Lord of
hosts will brandish a whip over them as when he struck
Midian at the rock of Oreb. And he will raise his stick over
27a, b the sea as he did against Egypt. And in that day Assyria's
burden will drop from your shoulders and his yoke will be
lifted from your neck.

Assyria moves swiftly towards Jerusalem—

27c Assyria has left Rimmon,
28 He has reached Aiath;
He has passed through Migron,
And left his baggage at Michmash;
29 They have crossed the ravine
And lodged for the night at Geba.
Ramah trembles in fear,
Gibeah of Saul is in full flight.
30 Cry out in alarm, daughter of Gallim,
Listen to her, Laishah,
Echo her cry, Anathoth!
31 Madmenah has fled,
The inhabitants of Gebim run for safety.

32   Today his halting-place is Nob,
      He will shake his fist
      At the Mount of the daughter of Zion,
      At the hill of Jerusalem.

—but the Lord can check his progress

33   Yet see, the Lord, the Lord of hosts,
      Will lop Assyria's boughs with fearful force.
      The tall trees will be hewn down,
      And the high and mighty will be brought low.
34   He will cut away the thickets of the forest,
      And the majestic cedars of Lebanon shall fall.

CHAPTER ELEVEN

The Prophet foresees the future king

1   Out of the felled stump of Jesse a shoot shall spring,
     Out of his roots a strong sapling shall rise.
2   Upon him will rest the Spirit of the Lord—
     The spirit of wisdom and insight,
     The spirit of just-dealing and power,
     The spirit of knowledge and reverence for the Lord.
3   He will not judge by appearances,
     He will not make decisions by hearsay;
4   But he will pronounce justice for the needy
     And make fair decisions for the poor.
     His verdicts will strike down the merciless
     And his pronouncements will be death to the wicked.
5   He will be girded around his waist with justice
     And with faithfulness around his loins.
6   The wolf shall live in peace with the lamb
     And the leopard will share his bed with the kid.
     The lion shall eat straw like an ox,
     While calf and young lion shall feed together;

86

And they will be herded by a little child.

7 The cow and the bear will be friends with each other
While their young shall nestle down together.

8 The suckling baby shall play over the hole of an asp
And the weaned child toddle around the viper's nest.

9 None shall hurt and none shall kill in all my holy mountain;
for the land shall be as full of the knowledge of the Lord as
the seas are filled with water.

The Prophet foretells the Lord's work of restoration

10 In that day the shoot of Jesse shall stand as a flag to rally the
peoples. The nations shall consult him and his dwelling-
place shall be famous.

11 In that day the Lord will again raise his hand to recover
the survivors of his people—from Assyria, from Egypt,
from Pathros, from Cush, from Elam, from Shinar, from
Hamath and from all the islands of the sea.

12 He will raise a standard for the nations
And he will gather together the outcasts of Israel.
He will bring in the scattered people of Judah
From the corners of the earth.

13 Envy of Ephraim will come to an end
And those who trouble Judah shall be destroyed.
Ephraim shall not be jealous of Judah
And Judah shall not trouble Ephraim.

14 But they shall both swoop down westwards on the
     Philistine's flank,
And together they shall plunder the people of the east.
Edom and Moab shall be brought under their power,
And the Ammonites shall do their bidding.

15 The Lord will parch the tongue of Egypt's sea,
He will raise his hand over the River
And strike it into seven dry gullies
Which men may cross in sandalled feet.

16 And there will be a high road from Assyria for the rest of his
people who are left there, as there was for Israel on the day
when they came up out of Egypt.

CHAPTER TWELVE

A psalm of thanksgiving in "that day"

1   In that day you will say:
I give thanks to you, Lord; for you were angry with me
And now your anger is past and you have given me
      comfort.
2   See, all my safety lies in God,
I trust him and know no fear!
The Lord is my strength and of him I sing,
He has become my saviour indeed!
3   Joyfully will you draw water from the wells of salvation.
4   And you will say in that day:
Give thanks to the Lord,
Call upon his name!
Make his deeds known among all nations,
Proclaim his name of majesty!
5   Sing the praises of the Lord, for he has done glorious
      things,
Let the whole earth know of it!
6   Shout aloud and sing for joy, you dwellers in Zion,
For great is the Holy One of Israel in your midst!

CHAPTER THIRTEEN

The coming destruction of Babylon

1 The fate of Babylon, clearly seen by Isaiah, the son of Amoz:

2 Raise the signal on a treeless hill,
Shout to them aloud;
Wave them on to enter
The gates of the aristocrats!

3 For I have charged my chosen men
To execute my anger,
Yes, I have called up my warriors,
My men of pride and joy.

4 Listen, a roar upon the mountains,
A sound of many people;
Listen, the noise of kingdoms,
Of nations gathering together.
For the Lord of hosts is mustering
A mighty army for battle.

5 They come from a land that is far away,
They come from distant horizons—
The Lord and the tools of his anger
To lay the whole earth waste.

6 Yell now in terror for the day of the Lord is near,
It comes as a mighty blow from the Almighty!

7 Therefore every hand will hang down helpless,
And the heart of every man shall fail,

8 And every mortal man shall be dismayed.
They shall be seized with pangs and pains,
They shall writhe like women in travail;
They shall stare at each other aghast,
Their faces red in the blaze.

9 For see, the day of the Lord comes,
Pitiless in anger and blazing with wrath,
To make the earth a desolation,

And destroy the sinners from its face.

10   For the stars of heaven, Orion and the constellations,
Shall fail to give their light;
The sun will be dark at its rising,
And the moon shall withhold its light.

God speaks

11   I will punish the world for its evil,
And the wicked for their sin;
I will break down the pride of the haughty
And lay the arrogance of the tyrant in the dust.

12   I will make mortals more rare than finest gold,
And men more scarce than the gold of Ophir!

The vision continues

13   Therefore shall the heavens tremble
And the earth be shaken from its place,
Because of the wrath of the Lord of hosts
In the day of his burning anger.

14   Then it shall be that like a hunted gazelle,
Like a flock of sheep with no shepherd,
Every man will turn to his own people,
Every man will run back to his own land.

15   Every one who is found shall be run through,
And every one who is caught shall die by the sword.

16   Before their eyes their children shall be dashed to
pieces,
Their houses stripped and their wives dishonoured.

God speaks again

17   I will stir up the Medes against them,
Men not swayed by silver
And who have no greed for gold;

18 But with bows and spears in their hands
Terrible and ferocious,
They cut young men to pieces,
With no mercy for the fruit of the womb,
Nor pity in their eyes for children.

The Prophet continues

19 Babylon, the crown of all kingdoms,
The pride and glory of the Chaldeans,
Shall become like Sodom and Gomorrah
When God destroyed them.
20 Never again shall it be inhabited,
From age to age no man shall dwell there;
There shall no Arab pitch his tent,
Nor shepherd feed his flock.
21 But wild dogs will lie down there,
And their houses shall be full of howling beasts.
There shall ostriches make their home,
And hairy wild goats dance.
22 Howling jackals shall sing in their halls
And wolves in their stately mansions.
Babylon's time is almost here,
Her days are surely numbered!

CHAPTER FOURTEEN

The restoration of Israel

1 For the Lord will deal gently with Jacob, and will choose
Israel once again. He will settle them in fields of their own.
A foreigner will come and live with them, and join the
2 household of Jacob. The house of Israel will be brought home
by other nations, and then, on the Lord's own acres, they
shall own these nations as slaves and slave-girls. Their captors
shall be their captives, and their task-masters shall be their
slaves.

3 Then it shall be that when the Lord has given you rest
from your toil and misery, from the hard labour which you
4a had to endure, then you will sing a song of contempt to the
king of Babylon, and you will say:

The end of tyranny

4b How has the Tyrant fallen,
And the Terror ceased to be!
5 The Lord has broken the staff of the wicked
And the sceptre of those who ruled,
6 Which struck the peoples in fury
With never-ending blows,
Which trod down the nations in anger,
In unrelenting wrath.
7 Now the whole earth lies quietly at peace,
And a song is on every lip.
8 The very cypresses are joyful,
The cedars of Lebanon cry aloud,
Since you were laid low,
None comes now to cut us down!

Excitement in the underworld

9   The underworld is all agog
To meet you when you come,
Summoning up ghosts for you—
Those who were leaders on earth;
Raising from their thrones
The kings of the nations
10   To greet you, one and all,
And say, So you too are as weak as we are,
You have become like one of us!
11   Your glory is brought down to the underworld
With all your sounds of music.
A mattress of maggots lies ready
With a blanket of worms to cover you.

The end of ambition

12   How you have fallen from heaven on high,
You shining son of the dawn!
How you are cut down to the ground,
You who laid all nations low!
13   You who once said in your heart,
I will scale the skies;
I will set up my throne on high
Above the stars of God,
That I may rule on the mount of the gods,
In the far high places of the North.
14   I will climb above the towering clouds
And be like God Most High!
15   Yet down to the underworld shall you be brought
To the dark, deep places of the Pit!

The final humiliation

16   The onlookers stare hard at you
Considering you with narrowed eyes—
Is this the man who caused the earth to tremble
And its kingdoms to quake in fear,

17   Who turned the world into a wilderness
And its cities into heaps of rubble,
Who never set a prisoner free
To go back to his home?

18   The kings of the nations sleep in glory,
Each in his own tomb;

19   But you are thrown out without a grave,
Like a hated monstrous birth,
Flung down among the corpses
Of the men who were slain by the sword,
Those who go down to the depths of the Pit,
A carcase under men's feet.

20a   You shall not join your fathers in the grave!

Why Babylon's king must be destroyed

20b   For you have ruined your country,
And destroyed your own people.
May the names of this evil man's sons
Never be heard upon earth!

21   Prepare his sons for slaughter,
To die for their father's guilt,
Lest they rise up and possess the earth,
And cover the world with their cities.

The Lord will wipe out Babylon

22   I will rise against Babylon, declares the Lord of hosts, and I
will wipe out both its name and its survivors, yes, both son

94

23 and grandson, says the Lord. I will turn it into pools of water and a haunt for the bittern; I will sweep it up with the broom of destruction, declares the Lord of hosts.

The Lord plans to destroy Assyria

24 The Lord of hosts has sworn an oath saying,
As I have planned, so shall it surely happen,
As I have purposed, so shall it surely be;
25 I will break Assyria on my own ground
And trample him upon my mountains;
His yoke shall be lifted from my people,
And his burden from their shoulders.
26 This is the plan which has been planned for the whole earth,
And this is the hand which is stretched out before all nations;
27 For the Lord of hosts has made his plan, who can unmake it?
The outstretched hand is his hand, who can turn it back?

The doom of Philistia

28 In the year that king Ahaz died there came this Warning:

29 Do not rejoice, any of you Philistines,
Because the stick that beat you has been broken;
For from its root a viper shall rise
Which will give birth to a flying serpent.
30 The poorest of the poor shall feed in my pasture,
And the needy will lie down in safety;
But what is left of you I will starve to death
And your survivors will I kill.
31 Yell in your towns! Shriek in your cities!
Let every Philistine faint for fear!
For smoke is rising in the north,
And the invader's ranks are closed.

32   And what answer will you give
      To the envoys of that nation?
      That the Lord is the founder of Zion
      And she is the refuge for his people in distress.

CHAPTER FIFTEEN

The doom of Moab

1   Because Ar fell at a blow, Moab is ruined;
     Because Kir fell at a blow, Moab is ruined.
2   The daughter of Dibon climbs up to her sacred places to
           weep,
     On the heights of Nebo and Medeba Moab wails aloud;
     Every head is shaved in sorrow, every beard is clipped.
3   In the streets they have put on sackcloth,
     On the rooftops and in the squares everyone wails—
     They are broken up with sorrow.
4   Heshbon and Elealeh cry out in distress
     And their cries are heard in Jahaz.
     Therefore the heart of Moab trembles
     And his soul shudders within him.
5   My heart cries out for Moab,
     For his fugitives flee to Zoar.
     They make the ascent of Luhith in tears,
     They wend their way to Horonaim
     Crying of their ruin.
6   For the waters of Nimrim are a barren waste,
     The grass is withered, the young growth fails
     And there is no green thing left.
7   Therefore the flock they have kept
     And all that they have saved
     They carry over the Brook of Willows.
8   Their cry rings through the length and breadth of Moab,
     Their wailing reaches Eglaim,
     Their wailing reaches Beer-elim,

9   For the waters of Dibon run with blood.
(Yet I will bring even more upon Moab—
A lion to attack those who escape,
The survivors of the land.)[1]

CHAPTER SIXTEEN

Moab seeks sanctuary in Judah

1   Then from Sela, by the desert road,
They shall send lambs as gifts to the ruler,
To the mountain of the daughter of Zion;
2   Like fluttering birds, like scattered nestlings,
The daughters of Moab will gather at the fords of Arnon,
      crying,
3   Give us advice, settle our affairs;
Shelter us with deep darkness in the noonday,
Hide away the outcasts, never betray the fugitives.
4a   Let the outcasts of Moab find refuge with you,
Shelter them from the fury of the destroyer.

The tyranny shall cease—

4b   When the oppressor is no more and destruction has ended,
When the trampler under foot is finished and gone,
5   Then in kindness shall your throne be set up,
In the very tent of David;
And on it shall sit in faithfulness,
A judge who seeks what is right
And is swift to execute justice.

—but Moab's pride leads to his destruction

6   But we have heard of the pride of Moab,
Of how very proud he is;

[1] The text here is uncertain.

Of his arrogance, his overbearing insolence,
Of all his empty boasting!
7   So Moab is left to wail for Moab,
The whole of Moab wails.
They moan for the raisin-cakes of Kir-hareseth
In utter misery.
8   For the fields of Heshbon are wilting
And the vine of Sibmah,
Whose grapes once mastered the rulers of the world
Which once stretched north to Jazer,
And spread to the desert in the south,
9   With tendrils pushing out to pass over the sea.
So I join with Jazer,
To weep for the vine of Sibmah.
Heshbon and Elealeh,
I drench you with my tears!
For the cries of battle have fallen
Upon your fruits and upon your harvest;
10   Joy and gladness vanish
From the land of happy fields.
No songs are sung in the vineyards,
No voices raised in joy.
No man treads wine from the grapes,
The vintage-shouts are silenced.
11   Therefore my pity for Moab is stirred within me
And the strings of my heart are plucked like a harp.

12 Even though Moab presents himself and wearies himself upon the high place; even when he comes into his sanctuary to pray, it will be to no avail.
13   This was the message which the Lord spoke about Moab
14 in the past. But now the Lord speaks, saying, In three years' time, no more no less, the glory of Moab will be a mockery, despite his teeming numbers. And few and feeble will be his survivors.

CHAPTER SEVENTEEN

Disaster follows forgetfulness of the Lord

1   Damascus, beware!
    Soon shall Damascus cease to be a city,
2   And lie in ruins, deserted for ever.
    Sheep shall take possession of her towns
    And lie down with none to scare them away.
3   Ephraim shall lose her protection
    And the royal power shall pass from Damascus.
    The survivors of Syria shall perish—
    Like the glory of the sons of Israel.
    This is the warning of the Lord of hosts!
4   The day shall come
    When the prosperity of Jacob shall wane,
    And his fat be reduced to leanness!
5   It will be like the time when the reaper has cut the standing
        grain
    And has gathered the ears in his arms in the rich valley of
        Rephaim;
6   Or when the olive-tree is beaten, and mere gleanings are
        left—
    Two or three berries on the topmost branch,
    Four or five left on the boughs.
    This is the warning of the Lord God of Israel!
9   In that day shall your cities be deserted,
    Like the ruins left by the Amorites and Hivites
    When they fled before the children of Israel,
    And they will become a desolation,
10 Because you have forgotten the God of your salvation
    And have not remembered the Rock which is your
        refuge,
    Although you may plant pretty little gardens,
    Stocking them with cuttings of an alien god;

11 Although you may make them grow on the day of
      planting,
And force them to blossom on the following day,
When the day comes to reap your harvest
It will vanish in pain which cannot be cured.

7 On that day man shall look to his Maker,
His eyes will turn to the Holy One of Israel.

8 He will look no longer on the work of his hands
Nor regard what his own fingers have made.

The power of man is nothing before the Lord

12 Hear the roar of many peoples
Roaring like the roaring seas!
Hear the surge of mighty nations
Like the surge of many waters!

13 They may roar like roaring waters
But the Lord has but to speak against them
And they are scattered far and wide,
Driven like chaff before the wind on the mountains,
Swirling like dust before the storm—

14 Terrible to behold in the evening
And gone without trace in the morning!
Such is the fate of those who plunder our goods,
Such is the lot of those who steal our wealth!

CHAPTER EIGHTEEN

The envoys of Ethiopia are sent back

1   Hı! You land of buzzing insects
Beyond the Ethıopian waters,
2   Which sends envoys down the Nile
In light skiffs on its stream!
Return, you swift messengers,
To a people fine-drawn and smooth,
A terror far and wıde,
A nation strong in conquest
Whose land is veined with rivers!

Men must know that the Lord is in control

3   Now, you inhabıtants of the world
And all who dwell upon earth:
When the signal is raised on the mountaın, watch!
When the trumpet is sounded, lısten!
4   For the Lord has saıd this to me:
I wıll watch from my dwelling-place
Quiet as the dazzling heat in the sunshine
Or as dew which falls in the time of harvest.
5   For before the harvest, when the blossom is over
And the grape is becoming ripe,
The branches shall be lopped off with pruning-hooks
And the spreadıng tendrils cut away.
6   Then shall they be left to vultures on the mountains
And to the wild beasts of the land.
They will be a summer feast for carrion bırds
And winter food for all wild beasts.

7 Then shall gifts be brought as tribute to the Lord of hosts,

From a people fıne-drawn and smooth,
A terror far and wide,

A nation strong in conquest,
Whose land is veined with rivers,

to mount Zion, the place of the name of the Lord of hosts.

CHAPTER NINETEEN

Egypt will disintegrate through civil war

1   Egypt, beware!
See, the Lord comes down to Egypt,
Riding swiftly upon a cloud;
The idols of Egypt will tremble at his presence,
And the courage of the Egyptian will melt away.

2   I will spur on Egyptian against Egyptian,
And they shall fight,
Every man against his brother,
Every man against his neighbour.
City against city, and kingdom against kingdom.

3   The very wits of Egypt shall be scattered
And I will make havoc of their plans;
They will resort to idols and magicians,
To wizards and to mediums.

4   And I will put the Egyptians under the power of a hard
      master,
And a fierce king shall dominate them.
This is what the Lord, the Lord of hosts, declares.

Egypt's river will be dried up

5   The waters of the Nile shall be dried up,
And the river-bed shall be drained dry;

6   The canals will shrink and grow foul
And the streams of the Nile shall dwindle.
Reeds and rushes will rot,

7   And the grass on its banks will wither.
All that is sown by the river shall be parched,

It will be blown away and be seen no more.

8   The fishermen shall mourn and lament—
All those who cast their hooks in the Nile
And those who spread their nets upon its waters.

9   Those who work in fine flax will be at their wits' end,
And those who weave white cotton.

10 For the pillars of society will be ruined
And the working men shall be in despair.

Egypt's wisdom is reduced to confusion

11 The princes of Zoan[1] are utterly witless,
Pharaoh's wisest planners make the silliest plans.
How can you say to Pharaoh,
A son of the wise am I, a son of ancient kings?

12 Where are your wise men, then, who can tell you
And let you know what the Lord of hosts has planned
            against Egypt?

13 The princes of Zoan are bemused,
The princes of Memphis are deluded,
And the leading men in her tribes have led Egypt astray.

14 The Lord has so addled their wits within them
That they make Egypt stagger in all her ways
As a drunkard staggers vomiting.

15 Nothing is being done in Egypt
From top to bottom, by palm or reed.

Egypt's terror of Judah, and her conversion to the Lord

16 In that day the Egyptians will become like women, and
tremble with fear as the hand of the Lord of hosts swings

17 over them. And the land of Judah will become a terror to the
Egyptians and the very mention of it will make them dread
what the Lord of hosts has planned against them.

[1] Egypt's summer capital, near the border of Palestine, and therefore
the court best known to Isaiah.

18   In that day there will be no less than five cities in the land
of Egypt speaking the language of Canaan and owing
allegiance to the Lord of hosts, and one of these cities will be
called the City of Righteousness.

19   In that day there will be an altar to the Lord in the centre
20 of Egypt and a pillar set up to him on her frontier. This will
be a reminder and a witness to the Lord of hosts in the land
of Egypt. When they cry to the Lord because of their oppressors he will send them a deliverer who will be their
21 champion and will rescue them. And the Lord will make
himself known to the Egyptians, and in that day the Egyptians will know the Lord. They will worship him with
sacrifice and offering; they will make vows to the Lord and
22 they will honour them. And the Lord will strike Egypt, both
striking and healing, and they will return to the Lord. He
will hear their prayers and heal them.

23   In that day there will be a highroad from Egypt to
Assyria so that the Assyrian will come into Egypt and the
Egyptian will go into Assyria. Egyptians and Assyrians
will worship the Lord together.

24   In that day Israel will form a triple alliance with Egypt
and Assyria, a source of blessing at the heart of the world,
25 blessed by the Lord of hosts when he said, Blessed be Egypt
my people, Assyria my handiwork and Israel who belongs
to me.

CHAPTER TWENTY

Egypt and Ethiopia are to be captured by Assyria

1 The Lord spoke to Isaiah the son of Amoz, saying, Go and
take off your sackcloth and throw off your shoes. Isaiah
2 obeyed, walking half-clad and barefoot. Then in the year
when the commander-in-chief, sent by Sargon, the king of
Assyria, came to Ashdod and both attacked and conquered
3 it, the Lord said, As my servant Isaiah has walked half-clad
and barefoot for three years as a sign and a warning against
4 Egypt and Ethiopia, so shall the king of Assyria lead away
captives from Egypt and exiles from Ethiopia. They will be
both young and old, and they will go half-clad, barefoot
5 with their buttocks exposed, to the shame of Egypt. Then
they will be dismayed and ashamed because of the hopes
they had had of Ethiopia and of the boasts they had made of
6 Egypt. In that day those who live in the lands by the sea will
say, If this is what has happened to those in whom we
trusted, those to whom we turned for rescue from the king
of Assyria, what chance of escape have we?

CHAPTER TWENTY-ONE

The Prophet's terrifying vision of Babylon's ruin

1a   A Warning from the desert:
2a   A dreadful vision has come to me,
1b   Roaring out of the desert
     From the terrible land,
     Sweeping on like the whirlwinds in the south.
2b   The plunderer continues his plundering,
     The destroyer continues his destruction.
     Up then, men of Elam, Besiege them, men of Media!
     Put an end to their boastings.

3   This is why I writhe in agony,
Pangs have seized me like a woman in labour,
I am stunned by what I hear,
I am aghast at what I see,

4   My mind reels,
My own shuddering appals me;
My longed-for evenings
Are filled with terrors.

5   They are arranging the tables,
They are spreading the rugs,
They are eating, they are drinking!
On your feet, you princes,
And put oil on your shields!

6   For the Lord has spoken these words to me,
Go and post a look-out,
Let him report whatever he sees.

7   If he sees riders,
Horsemen in pairs,
Riders on asses
Or riders on camels,
Then let him watch closely,
As a lion watches his prey.

8   Then he cried,
Lord, here am I, standing at my look-out
Continually by day,
Here am I stationed at my post
Through all the nights.

9   And, see, here come riders,
Horsemen in pairs!
And then he went on,
Babylon has fallen, fallen,
And all her idols lie shattered on the ground.

10   My own people, threshed and beaten
Like grain upon the threshing floor,
What I tell you now is what I have heard
From the Lord of hosts, the God of Israel.

The question from Edom

11   Dumah, beware!
Someone is crying out to me from Seir,
Watchman, how much of the night is gone?
Watchman, how much of the night is gone?
12   The watchman said,
Morning comes, and the night too.
If you want to know more
Come back and ask again.

13   Arabia, beware!
You must spend the night in the woods
You caravans of Dedanites.
14   Bring water for the thirsty,
Men of the land of Tema,
Bring food for the fugitives—
15   For they have fled from the sword,
From the sharpened sword, the bent bow
And the long weariness of battle.

16   For the Lord says this to me:
Within a year, neither more nor less,
The whole glory of Kedar will be finished.
17   And of Kedar's great army of archers
Few shall be left.
This is what the Lord, the God of Israel, has said.

CHAPTER TWENTY-TWO

The people rejoice; the Prophet sees disaster

1   A Warning from the valley of vision:
     What do you mean by going up,
     Crowding on to the house-tops
2   With shouts of joy on your lips—
     A city in an uproar,
     A town of celebration?
     Your dead were not killed by the sword,
     They did not die in battle.
3   All your leaders took to their heels
     And were caught without bows in their hands.
     Every man who fled was captured,
     However far he ran.

4   Therefore I say, Leave me alone,
     Let me weep bitter tears,
     Stop trying to console me,
     For all my people are wiped out.

5   For the Lord God of hosts has a day
     Of panic and trampling and confusion
     In the valley of vision—
     The battering down of walls
     And cries for help resounding from the mountains.
6   Elam took up the quiver
     With chariots and horsemen,
     And Kir unsheathed the sword.
7   Your fairest valleys were filled with chariots,
     And horsemen stood ready before the gates.
8   Judah's defences are down!

    In that day you looked to the trees of the forest for defence
9 as you saw the many gaps in the walls of David's city. You

10 collected water in the lower pool; you listed the houses of
Jerusalem, and demolished some of them to strengthen the
11 wall. You made a reservoir between the two walls to hold
water from the old pool. But you did not lift your eyes to
him who made these things happen, nor did you pay heed
to him who planned them long ago.

Judah's unpardonable gaiety

12   In that day the Lord God of hosts will call for tears and
mourning,
For shaven heads and wearing sackcloth.
13   And look, there is laughter and merry-making!
The killing of oxen and the slaughtering of sheep,
Eating meat and drinking wine;
Eating and drinking! Tomorrow we may die!
14   The Lord of hosts has told me this, his very voice in my
ear:
Surely you will not be forgiven for this sin until you die.

The disgrace of Shebna and his replacement by Eliakim

15 This is what the Lord God of hosts says: Come, go to
Shebna, this steward over the royal household, and say,
16 What right have you to be here, what family do you
possess that you should hew out a tomb for yourself here?
Why should you hew out your tomb on the height and
17 carve out a house for yourself in the rock? See, you mighty
man, the Lord will send you hurtling through the air—
18 he will take firm hold of you, roll you up into a ball and
hurl you into a vast and distant land. There you shall die and
there you shall have your glorious tomb, you disgrace to
19 your master's house! I will depose you from your office and
20 drag you down from where you stand. In that day I will call
21 my servant Eliakim, the son of Hilkiah, and clothe him
with your robe and tie round him your girdle and I will put

your authority into his hand and he shall become a father to
22 those who live in Jerusalem and to the house of Judah. I will
put the key of the house of David upon his shoulder, and
when he opens no man can shut, and when he shuts no man
23 can open. And I will make him secure, like a peg driven
firmly home, and he will bring great honour to his father's
24 house. Then the whole weight of his family will hang upon
him, relatives and dependents, all the common vessels from
25 cups to pitchers. And when this has happened, says the Lord
of hosts, the peg that was firmly driven home will give way;
it will be wrenched out and will fall, and the burden which
hung upon it will come crashing down. This is what the
Lord says.

CHAPTER TWENTY-THREE

Tyre and Sidon are doomed

1   A Warning about Tyre:
Weep and wail, you ships of Tarshish,
For your harbour is destroyed,
(As they sailed home from Cyprus
They were told the news.)
2   The men who live by the coast are struck dumb,
Those merchants of Sidon who sailed the seas,
And traded in many waters,
3   Harvesters of Egypt's grain
Who won their wealth from world-wide trade.

4   Weep for shame, Sidon, for the sea is saying,
I have not been in labour,
I have not given birth;
And I have reared no young men
Nor brought up any maidens!
5   (When the news reaches Egypt
There will be anguish at the fate of Tyre.)

6   Go over to Tarshish and wail
     You who live by the sea;
7   Is this your carefree city
     Founded in days of old,
     Whose feet, in days gone by,
     Carried her settlers far and wide?
8   Who has planned such a thing
     Against Tyre, that queen of cities,
     Whose merchants were princes among men,
     And whose traders were the envy of the world?
9   The Lord of hosts has planned it,
     To rob their pride of all its glory
     And dishonour what is honoured upon earth.

10   Now flow out over your lands, Tarshish,
     For the barriers are no more!
11   For the Lord has stretched out his hand against the
       sea
     And has made the kingdoms tremble.
     He has issued an order against Canaan
     That her strong forts should be destroyed;
12   He has said, You shall exult no more,
     You ravished daughter of Sidon!
     Rise and cross over to Cyprus;
     Even there you will find no rest.

13 Look at the land of the Chaldeans, a nation no longer; the
Assyrians have made it fit for the beasts of the desert. They
destroyed its cities; they set up their earthworks and ruined
its defences.

14   Weep and wail, you ships of Tarshish,
     For your harbour is destroyed
     And you have no port to enter.

15 In that day, Tyre shall be forgotten for seventy years, for

the lifetime of a king. Tyre will be like the harlot in the ditty:

16   Take up your harp,
      Mix with the throng,
      Harlot forgotten by men.
      Use all your art,
      Sing us your song,
      And you'll be remembered again!

17 At the end of seventy years the Lord will restore Tyre and she will return to her business and she will traffic with all
18 the kingdoms of the world upon the face of the earth. The proceeds of her trade shall be dedicated to the Lord; they shall not be stored up nor hoarded, but what she has gained shall provide food in abundance and clothes of splendour for the people of the Lord.

CHAPTER TWENTY-FOUR

The Judgement to come

1   See, the Lord is swilling out the earth and leaving it
          empty;
      He will crumple its surface and scatter its inhabitants!
2   There will be no difference
      Between priest and people,
      Master and slave,
      Mistress and maid,
      Seller and buyer,
      Borrower and lender,
      Creditor and debtor.
3   The earth shall be utterly empty,
      The world shall be stripped bare;
      For this is what the Lord has said.
4   The earth droops and withers,
      The world wilts and withers,

112

The high heavens wilt with the earth!
5   The earth has grown polluted through its people,
Because they have flouted laws, violated statutes
And broken the eternal covenant.

6   Therefore the earth is under a curse
And its people are paying the price.
Therefore the men upon earth are parched
And those who are left are few.

7   The wine fails, the vine is withered;
The merry-makers sigh in sorrow,

8   The joyful tambourines are silent,
The shouts of the revellers have died away,
And the happy notes of the harp are still.

9   There is no more singing as they drink the wine
And strong drink is bitter to those who drink it.

10   The city is in chaos, fallen and broken,
Every house is barred so that none can enter,

11   In the streets they shout for wine.
Darkness is falling on joy after joy
And laughter is banished from the earth.

12   The city is left desolate
And its gates are battered ruins.

13   The people who remain on earth will be few,
Few as the olives left when the tree has been beaten,
Few as the gleanings of grapes when the vintage is done.

The time for rejoicing is not yet

14   They lift up their voices, they sing for joy;
They cry aloud from the sea at the majesty of the Lord.

15   Therefore glorify the Lord in eastern lands,
And praise the name of the Lord, the God of Israel, on
    western shores.

16   From the ends of the earth we hear songs of praise,
Glory for the righteous!
But I say, I am wretched,

I am drawn with misery, for I see
Wicked men dealing wickedly,
Yes, wicked men dealing wickedly in wickedness.

17   Terror and pitfall and snare await you,
You who live on the earth!

18   The man who flees from the sound of terror
Shall fall into the pit,
And he who climbs up from the pit
Shall be caught in the snare.
For the windows of heaven are opened,
And the foundations of the earth are shaken.

19   The earth is broken in pieces,
The earth is split apart,
The earth is shaken to the core,

20   The earth staggers like a drunken man
And sways like a crazy shack.
Its sins lie heavy upon it,
And it falls to rise no more.

21   On that day the Lord will punish
The host of heaven in heaven
And the kings of the earth on earth.

22   They will be herded like prisoners in a cell
And penned together in prison,
And after many days they will be punished.

23   Then the moon shall veil her light
And the blaze of the sun grow pale,
For the Lord of hosts will be king in Mount Zion
And will reveal his glory before his elders in Jerusalem.

CHAPTER TWENTY-FIVE

A Song of Thanksgiving

1   O Lord, you are my God;
I will glorify you, I will sing the praises of your name;
For you have done marvellous things—
Plans formed long ago have been perfectly fulfilled.

2   You have turned a city into a pile of rubble,
And a fortified city into a heap of ruins.
The stronghold of the proud is a city no more
And it will never be rebuilt.

3   Therefore strong peoples recognise your might,
The cities of cruel nations hold you in awe.

4   You have been a refuge to the helpless,
A refuge for the needy in distress;
A shelter from the storm and a shade from the heat,
For the breath of cruel men is like a wintry blast.

5   As heat in a dry place is tempered by the shadow of a
      cloud,
So you subdue the shouts of the proud
And silence the songs of the cruel.

The bounty and pity of the Lord

6   And on this mountain the Lord of hosts will provide for
      all peoples
A banquet of rich food, a banquet of matured wine,
Of rich food full of goodness, of wine matured and
      refined.

7   And on this mountain he will destroy
The veil of sorrow which covers all peoples,
And the web which covers every nation.

8   He has swallowed up death forever,
And the Lord God will wipe away tears from all faces
And remove his people's shame from the whole earth.

For this is what the Lord says.

9 It will be said on that day,
See, this is our God;
We have waited for him to save us.
This is the Lord for whom we waited,
Let us rejoice and exult in his deliverance!

Yet Moab faces utter humiliation.

10 The hand of the Lord shall rest on this mountain,
And Moab shall be trampled down on his own land
As straw is trodden down in a dung-pit.

11 And he will spread out his hands in the midst of it
Like a swimmer spreading his hands to swim.
His pride will be laid low despite all his skill;

12 The high fortress of his walls will be brought down,
Laid low, thrown to the ground, reduced to dust.

CHAPTER TWENTY-SIX

A hymn of confidence in the Lord—

1 In that day this song shall be sung in the land of Judah:

We have a strong city,
Walled and buttressed by the Lord,
To keep us safe!

2 Open the gates for the righteous to enter,
The nation of loyal men!

3 You keep the steadfast man in perfect peace,
For in you is his sure confidence.

4 Trust in the Lord forever,
For the Lord God is everlasting and cannot be moved.

5 He has brought down those who live in the heights,
The city set up on high,
He brings it down to earth,
He lays it in the dust.

6   It is trodden underfoot
     By the feet of the poor,
     By the footsteps of the needy.

        —and a prayer of faith

7   The road of the righteous is a level road,
     You smooth out the way of the righteous.
8   We have waited in the path of your judgements, Lord,
     Longing in our hearts for a sign of you.
9   My soul longs for you in the night,
     Yes, I seek you with all my heart.
     For when your judgements descend upon the earth
     The inhabitants of the world learn what is right.
10   But if favour is shown to the wicked
     He does not learn to do right;
     Even in a land of justice he acts wickedly
     And fails to see the majesty of the Lord.
11   Lord, your hand is poised to strike, but they see nothing!
     Now let them see, to their confusion, your jealous care
           for your people.
     Let fire burn up those who would oppose you, O Lord,
12   But order for us peace and prosperity,
     For we recognise your hand in all our deeds.
13   O Lord, our God, other lords beside you have been our
           masters,
     But now it is your name only which we acknowledge.
14   They are dead men who live no more,
     They are ghosts who will never return.
     For you visited and destroyed them
     And wiped them from our memory.
15   You have swelled the ranks of our nation, Lord,
     You have shown us your glorious power;
     You have extended our borders on every side!
16   O Lord, in our distress we sought you,
     We cried out under the weight of trouble

117

When your chastening hand lay upon us.

17 As a pregnant woman writhes and cries out in her pangs
As her time draws near,
So were we in your presence, Lord.

18 We were in labour, we writhed in pain,
But we gave birth to nothing, nothing.
We could not keep our country safe
Nor defeat the men of the world around.

19 But your dead will live, their bodies will rise;
Those who live in the dust shall awake and sing for joy;
For your dew falls with glistening light
And the earth turns ghosts into men again!

The Lord's people must hide from the wrath of his judgement

20 Go now into your rooms, my people,
And shut your doors behind you.
Hide yourselves for a little while,
Until the storm has passed.

21 For see, the Lord leaves his heaven
To punish men upon earth for their sins.
Earth will reveal the blood shed upon her
And cover her corpses no more.

1 Then with his great sword, strong and grim,
The Lord will punish the serpent who flies,
And the serpent who crawls,
And he will slay the dragon who lives in the sea.

CHAPTER TWENTY-SEVEN

The Lord's people are under his constant care

2 Sing now a song of a pleasant vineyard:
3 I, the Lord, am guarding it,
  Hour by hour I water it,
  Day and night I guard it,
  Lest a single leaf be missing.
4 I have no wrath in my heart,
  But if there were thorns and briars
  I would do battle with them and crush them,
  I would burn them up together.
5 Cling to me for protection;
  Make peace with me,
  With me make peace!
6 The day will come when Jacob shall take root;
  Israel shall blossom and flourish,
  Till the whole world is filled with his fruit.

The Lord's punishment is not purposeless

7 Has he struck them as hard as he struck their oppressors?
  Have they known death as those who killed them have
    known it?
8 He has dealt with them by dismissing them, by banishing
    them,
  He has driven them away by his fierce blast,
  Like the scorching wind from the desert.
9 Yet only in this way shall the guilt of Jacob be removed,
  And only thus can the fruit of his forgiveness be shown;
  They must smash their stone altars into pounded chalk,
  And leave no sacred pole or incense altar standing.
10 For the fortified city is desolate,
  A house deserted and forsaken as the desert.
  There grazes a calf,

There he lies down, there he nibbles the branches.
11 When the boughs are dry they break
And women come and use them for firewood.
For this is a people with no eyes to see;
Therefore their maker shows them no mercy,
And their Creator shows them no kindness.

Yet again the promise of final restoration

12 In that day the Lord will thresh out the grain from the
river Euphrates to the brook of Egypt. And you will be
picked up one by one, you people of Israel. In that day a
great trumpet will sound, and those who were lost in the
land of Assyria and those who were outcasts in the land of
Egypt will come and worship the Lord on the holy mountain in Jerusalem.

CHAPTER TWENTY-EIGHT

The Prophet condemns the dissolute nobility

1 Why this crown of pride on Ephraim's drunken head!
Why the glorious beauty of frail flowers
Which wreathe the fertile valley,
Whose owners lie dead drunk!
2 Beware! The Lord's agent is strong and powerful,
Like a storm of hail, a hurricane of havoc,
Like a torrent of rain, flooding and flattening,
Flung down with fury upon the earth!
3 The crown of pride on Ephraim's drunken head
Shall be trampled underfoot,
4 And the glorious beauty of frail flowers
Which wreathe the fertile valley
Shall be like the first ripe fig of the season,
Seen, seized and swallowed all in a moment!

What will be—and what is!

5 In that day the Lord of hosts shall himself be a crown of
        glory
   And a diadem of beauty for the survivors of his people.
6 He will give wisdom to those who sit in judgement
   And strength to those who defend the gate.
7 Yet here in Jerusalem men reel with wine
   And stagger with strong drink.
   Priest and prophet reel in their cups,
   They are befuddled with wine,
   They stagger with strong drink,
   Their very visions are distorted,
   They stumble over their words of judgement.
8 The sacred tables are covered with filthy vomit,
   There is not a place that is clean.

The revellers mock the Prophet—

9 Who is he trying to teach?
   Who is he trying to instruct?
   Are we just weaned,
   Are we children just taken from the breast,
10 Do we have to learn that
   The-law-is-the-law-is-the-law,
   The-rule-is-the-rule-is-the-rule,
   A little bit here, a little bit there?

—and he replies

11 Yes, with stuttering lips and a foreign tongue
   Will the Lord speak to this people.
12 He once said to them:
   This is the rest you may give to the weary,
   This is the true refreshing,
   And yet they would not hear.

13 (So the word of the Lord shall be to them:
The-law-is-the-law-is-the-law,
The-rule-is-the-rule-is-the-rule,
A little bit here, a little bit there.[1])
So they go stumbling backwards,
To be broken and trapped and captured.

It is time to stop mockery and face reality

14 Therefore listen to the word of the Lord, you scoffers
Who rule this people in Jerusalem!

15 Because you say, We have struck a bargain with death,
We have made an agreement with the underworld,
When the overwhelming flood passes through
It will not reach us,
For we have hidden behind a lie
And taken refuge behind deceit;

16 Therefore this is what the Lord God says:
Here I lay the foundation of Zion,
A stone, a well-tested stone,
A precious corner stone, solid and secure:
The man who trusts in me shall rest unmoved.

17 I will make justice my line
With righteousness its plummet;
Then hail will sweep away the refuge of lies
And floods will overwhelm your shelter.

18 Then your bargain with death will be cancelled,
And your agreement with the underworld broken.
When the overwhelming flood passes through
You will be beaten down by it;

19 Every time it sweeps through it will take some of you,
Morning after morning it will surge through
By day and by night;
All news will be of unspeakable terror.

20 The bed is indeed too short for comfort

[1] The manuscript evidence for this part of the verse is uncertain.

And the blanket too narrow for warmth!

21   For the Lord will rise up as he did on Mount Perazim,
He will be angry as he was in the valley of Gibeon;
That he may do his deed, strange though it be,
And work his work, strange as it is.

22   Now, therefore, stop your mockery
Or you will be bound more fast than ever.
For I have heard from the Lord God of hosts
An order for destruction of the whole land.

Can men not learn from the methods of the farmer?

23   Now listen closely to my words,
Hear what I have to say! ·

24   Does the ploughman do nothing but plough,
Is he always opening and breaking down his ground?

25   Surely, once the field is smooth and level,
Does he not broadcast the dill and scatter the cummin,
And plant the wheat and barley in rows,
With vetches sown as a border?

26   For he is instructed aright
And taught by his God.

27   Dill is not threshed with a threshing sledge,
Nor is a cart-wheel rolled over cummin!
But dill is threshed with a stick,
And cummin with a flail.

28   No one crushes bread-corn to pieces;
But once the cart-wheel has been driven over it
A man spreads it out and does not crush it.

29   This knowledge also comes from the Lord of hosts,
Whose counsel is wonderful, and whose wisdom is
great.

CHAPTER TWENTY-NINE

Jerusalem will be surrounded and marvellously rescued

1　Jerusalem, God's hearth and altar,
　　Where David set up his camp!
　　Let year follow year,
　　Let the round of festivals continue;
2　Yet I will bring trouble upon this hearth and altar,
　　And there will be groaning and grief,
　　And she shall truly be an altar burning for me!
3　I will encircle you with an armed camp,
　　I will surround you with towers of battle
　　And hem you in with siege-works.
4　Then you will speak as you lie prostrate,
　　Your words will come humbly from the earth,
　　And weak as the voice of a ghost
　　Will be your squeaking from the dust!
5　But the army of your enemies shall become like fine dust,
　　And the army of the ruthless shall be scattered like chaff
　　　　in the wind.
　　For suddenly, in the twinkling of an eye,
6　You will be visited by the Lord of hosts
　　With thunder and earthquake and dreadful noise,
　　With storm and whirlwind and consuming fire.
7　The whole horde of nations who take arms against
　　　　Jerusalem,
　　Yes, all who besiege and oppress her
　　Shall vanish away like a dream of the night.
8　As when a hungry man dreams he is eating
　　And wakes still hungry,
　　Or a thirsty man dreams he is drinking
　　And wakes with his thirst unquenched,
　　So shall it be with the armies of all nations
　　Who fight against Mount Zion.

The Prophet declares the blindness of the nation to the truth

9   Stupefy yourselves, yes, live in a stupor,
    Blind yourselves, yes, live in darkness!
    Fuddle your wits, but not with wine!
    Stagger about, but not through drink!
10 For the Lord has drowned you in deepest sleep;
    He has closed the eyes of the prophets,
    And muffled the heads of the seers,
11 So that the word of the Lord
    Is a closed book to you.

12 (When men give it to a learned man and ask him to read
    it he says, I cannot, it is a closed book. When they give it to
    the illiterate and ask him to read it, he says, I cannot read.)

The Lord plans a salutary shock for his people

13 Now the Lord says:
    Because this people draws near to me only in words
    And honours me with no more than lip-service,
    While their hearts are far from me,
    And their reverence for me is a rule they have learned by
        heart;
14 See, I will deal with them in a way that will astonish them
    And leave them filled with amazement and wonder!
    For the wisdom of their wise men shall be eclipsed
    And the understanding of their clever men be over-
        shadowed.

God is the master, not man

15 Alas for those who hide their plans from the Lord,
    Whose deeds are done in the dark;
    Who say, Who sees us? Who knows what we do?
16 Your thoughts are upside down—

Is the potter so much clay?
Is the thing that is made to say to its maker,
He did not make me?
Can the pot say of the potter,
He has no sense?

There will be confusion—

17 It shall surely not be long before
Lebanon's forests turn into fertile fields,
And fertile fields become like forests!

—before final restoration

18 But in that day the deaf shall hear words from a book,
And out of their darkness and gloom
The eyes of the blind shall see.
19 The humble shall find new joy in the Lord,
And the poor among men shall rejoice in the Holy One of
Israel.
20 For the tyrant's day shall be over and the scoffer be no
more.
All who watched for evil will be wiped out—
21 Those who destroyed a man with a single word,
Who perverted the course of justice,
And defrauded the innocent by a legal quibble.

*The Lord's people will eventually honour him for all that
he has done*

22 Therefore the Lord, who rescued Abraham, says this con-
cerning Jacob's house:

Never again shall Jacob be disgraced,
Never shall his face grow pale in fear.
23 For when his children have seen
All that I have done for them,

They will honour my name,
They will honour the Holy One of Jacob,
And will stand in awe of the God of Israel.

24 Those who have been faithless will understand the truth
And the obstinate be willing to be taught.

CHAPTER THIRTY

A warning against the treaty with Egypt

1 Alas for you, you rebellious children, says the Lord,
Who carry out a plan which is none of mine,
Who weave an alliance without my blessing,
And so add sin to sin;

2 Who set out to go to Egypt,
Without seeking any word from me,
To seek the protection of Pharaoh
And shelter in the shadow of Egypt.

3 For the protection of Pharaoh shall prove a humiliation,
And sheltering in the shadow of Egypt shall prove your
    undoing.

4 For though he has princes at Zoan
And his messengers reach Hanes,

5 Everyone shall be ashamed of a nation who is no use to
    them,
Who can give neither help nor profit
But only disillusion and disgrace.

The dangerous and useless journey to Egypt

6 They go through the heat of the Southland,
Through a land of drought and anguish,
The home of the lion and lioness,
The viper and the flying serpent.
They carry their riches on the backs of asses,
And their treasures on the humps of camels,

127

To a people who can be of no use to them.

7   For Egypt's help is empty and worthless;
This is why I call her the Spent Whirlwind.

The Prophet must record the people's faithlessness

8   And now, go in and inscribe this on a tablet
And write it on a scroll,
To serve as a lasting witness
In all the days to come.

9   For they are a rebellious people,
Sons who dishonour their father,
Children who refuse to hear the teaching of the Lord,

10   Who say to the seers, See nothing,
And to the prophets, Never tell us what is right.
Speak to us pleasant words, prophesy illusions!

11   Get out of our way, leave our path clear,
Let us hear no more of the Holy One of Israel!

Refusal to trust the Lord will mean disaster

12   Therefore the Holy One of Israel says this:
Because you have spurned this warning
And put your faith in force and intrigue
And have come to rely on them,

13   This guilt of yours will be like the crack
Which runs down the bulge of a collapsing wall,
Whose crash comes suddenly, in an instant;

14   Like an earthen pot which is smashed beyond repair,
So that among the fragments
Not a single piece can be found
Big enough to carry fire from the hearth
Or to scoop water from the well.

15   For the Lord God, the Holy One of Israel, has said:
In returning and in rest shall you be saved;
In quietness and confidence shall be your strength.

But you would not agree;
16   Instead you answered,
No, we must have horses to ride.
Very well, you shall ride—in full retreat!
We must have swift horses, you say;
Your pursuers will be swifter still!
17   A thousand shall flee at the threat of one man
And ten thousand at the threat of five,
Till you are left
Like a flagstaff on top of a mountain
Or a beacon high on a hill.

A promise of forgiveness and prosperity

18   The Lord is waiting to deal kindly with you;
His mercy is not yet shown.
For the Lord is a God of justice,
Happy are those who wait patiently for him!

19 You people in Zion, who live in Jerusalem, you shall weep no more. For he will be gracious to you when he
20 hears your cry; and when he hears he will answer you. Even though the Lord has given you the bread of adversity and the water of affliction, yet your Teacher will no longer be hidden away in a corner; you will keep your eyes on your
21 Teacher for guidance. And when you might turn to the left or to the right, your ears will hear the words of your
22 Guide saying, This is the path; follow it! Then you will be revolted by the silver-covered images which you have carved and the gold-plated images which you have cast. You will throw them away like dirty rags. Good riddance, you will say, to bad rubbish!
23   Then he will send rain for the seed which you will sow in the ground, and the wheat, the fruit of the soil, will be rich and plentiful. On that day your cattle will graze freely in
24 their pastures, and the oxen and young asses which till the

ground shall be fed with salted fodder made from winnowed
25 and shovelled grain. And on every lofty mountain and on
every high hill there will be streams running with water.
26 The moonlight will be as bright as sunshine, and the sun
will shine seven times more brightly, giving seven days'
light in one, on the day when the Lord binds up the bruises
of his people and heals the wounds which his blows have
inflicted.

But the Lord is terrible in judgement

27   See, the Lord himself comes from afar
    Blazing with anger, glorious in majesty!
    His lips are filled with fury, and his tongue like devouring
      fire;
28   His coming is like a river in spate
    Flooding up to a man's neck.
    He comes to riddle the nations in the sieve of destruction,
    And to place in the jaws of the peoples
    A bit that will lead them to their doom.

Various prophecies of divine retribution[1]

30 The Lord will make men hear the voice of his majesty and
make them see his arm descending to strike in fury, in a
flame of devastating fire, in a cloudburst, in a hurricane and
31 a storm of hail. The Assyrians will be terror-stricken at the
voice of the Lord when they are struck by his rod, yes, at
32a every stroke of the staff of punishment which the Lord lays
upon them.
33   For a fire of destruction has long lain ready. Yes, it is fit
for a king, a pyre both deep and wide, piled up with straw
and logs in plenty! The breath of the Lord, like a stream of
25d,e burning sulphur, will set it ablaze. In the day when the
29 towers fall, in the day of the great massacre, you will sing a

---

[1] The verses from here to the end of Ch. 30 are obviously out of order.
I owe this re-arrangement to the Interpreter's Bible.

song such as you sing in the night when a holy feast is kept. You will know the gladness of heart which a man feels as he sets out with the sound of the flute to go to the mountain
32b of the Lord, to the Rock of Israel. To the sound of tambourines and lyres the Lord will do battle with the Assyrians and shake them till they die!

CHAPTER THIRTY-ONE

It is the Lord who can save, not Egypt!

1 Shame on those who go down to Egypt for help,
   Who rely on the power of horses,
   Who put their trust in the number of their chariots
   And in the strength of their cavalry;
   Who pay no heed to the Holy One of Israel
   Nor seek counsel from the Lord!
2 Yet he, too, can be relied on—to bring disaster!
   He does not call back his promises.
   He will rise up against the house of wicked men
   And against those who help the evildoers.
3 Egyptians are men and not God;
   Their horses are flesh and not spirit!
   When the Lord stretches out his hand,
   The helper will stumble and the helped will fall,
   And they will both perish together.
4 For this is what the Lord has said to me:
   As a lion or young lion growls over his prey,
   Yet when the shepherds are called out
   To band together to attack him,
   He is not terrified by their shouting
   Nor daunted by their noise,
   So shall the Lord of hosts come down
   To fight against Mount Zion and against its hill.

131

Return to the Lord means the rout of Assyria

5   As birds hover round their nests
    So the Lord of hosts will protect Jerusalem;
    He will shield her and save her,
    He will spare her and rescue her.
6   The people of Israel shall return to him
    From whom they have rebelled in their hearts.
7   For in that day each man will throw away
    The idols of silver and idols of gold,
    Which your own hands made for you.
8   And the Assyrian shall fall,
    But not by human sword,
    He will be struck down,
    But by no mortal blade;
    He will flee away, but not from the sword of man!
    His young men shall be sold into slavery,
9   In fear he will rush blindly past his stronghold,
    And his officers desert their flag in panic.
    This is what the Lord says,
    Whose fire is in Zion
    And whose furnace is in Jerusalem.

CHAPTER THIRTY-TWO

The Prophet declares what might be

1   If the king reigned in righteousness
    And the princes ruled with justice,
2   If both were a refuge from the wind
    And a shelter from the storm;
    If they were like running streams in a dry country,
    And like shadows of a great rock in a weary land;
3   If the eyes of those who can see were no longer turned
        away

132

And the ears that can hear were ready to listen,

4 If the mind of the hasty were ready to learn
And the tongue of the hesitant spoke clearly,

5 Then the decadent would no longer be called noble
Nor the crafty a man of worth.

6 For the decadent speaks decadence
And his mind is plotting mischief—
To live a godless life
And speak evil about the Lord,
To let the hungry man go hungry
And keep the thirsty short of water.

7 The crafty has evil crafty ways,
For he devises wicked plots
To ruin the needy with his lies,
Even when the poor man's cause is just.

8 But the noble man's plans are noble
And nobly does he stand by them.

The Prophet warns the careless women of Judah

9 Get up now, you carefree women,
And hear what I have to say!
You complacent maidens, listen to my speech!

10 For the day will come
When you will shudder, you carefree women;
For the vintage will fail
And there will be no fruit to gather.

11 Tremble, you carefree women,
Shudder, you complacent ones!
Strip, make yourselves naked,
Put on girdles of sackcloth.

12 Beat on your breasts in mourning
For the once pleasant fields, the once fruitful vine;

13 For the land of my people overgrown with thorns and
briars,
For all those happy houses,

For that city full of joy.
14 For the palace will be forsaken,
The bustling city deserted;
Hill and watch-tower will lie in ruins,
A stamping-ground for wild asses,
A pasture for the flocks,
15a Until there is poured upon us
The Spirit from on high.

Yet in the end there will be peace and security

15b Then the wilderness shall become a fertile field
And fertile fields become like forests.
16 Then justice will dwell in the wilderness
And righteousness will live in the fertile field.
17 And the fruit of righteousness shall be peace,
And the end of justice shall be quiet confidence forever.
18 And my people shall settle down in peace,
Living in safe houses, resting undisturbed—
19 No matter what forest is felled by hail,
No matter what city is razed to the ground.
20 In happiness you will sow by unfailing waters
And let the ox and the ass range free.

CHAPTER THIRTY-THREE

Treacherous Assyria will be destroyed

1 Hi! Killer not killed, and raider not raided;
When your killing is finished, you shall be killed;
When your raiding is finished, you shall be raided!

A prayer to the Lord

2 Lord, be gracious to us; our hope is in you.
Be our strength every morning

And our help in time of trouble.

3 At the noise of your thunder the peoples flee,
And in your silence men are scattered.

4 Like locusts they devour the spoil,
And swarm upon it like a swarm of grasshoppers.

5 The Lord is exalted, for he lives on high;
He has filled Zion with justice and goodness.

6 Wisdom and knowledge of him are her security,
And reverence for him is her treasure.

7 See, the priests wail far from their altar,
Envoys of peace weep bitterly,

8 The highways are in ruins,
No one travels.
Treaties are torn up,
Witnesses are disregarded,
Human rights are spurned.

9 The land is dry and withered,
Lebanon shrivels in shame,
Sharon has become a desert,
Bashan and Carmel have shaken off their leaves.

The Lord's warning to Assyria—and to all peoples

10 Now will I arise, says the Lord,
Now will I lift myself up,
Now will I be exalted!

11 Your plans are like stubble and chaff—
Fuel to the flames of your fury.

12 And the peoples shall be burnt to lime
As thorns cut down are burnt to ashes.

13 Now hear what I have done, you that are far away,
And you that are near acknowledge my might.

14 The sinners in Zion are afraid;
The godless are seized with terror—

Which of us can live with devouring fire?
Which of us can exist with eternal flame?
15 He who lives honestly and speaks sincerely,
Who scorns to profit by wronging others,
Who waves aside a bribe,
Who lends no ear to murderous plots
And contemplates no crime.
16 Such a man shall live above all harm,
Secure as someone in a rocky stronghold;
His bread provided, and his water sure.

Jerusalem's glorious future

17 Your eyes shall see the king in his beauty;
You will look round in a land of wide horizons,
18 And think of the days of tyranny, wondering,
Where is he who counted our goods?
Where is he who weighed our tribute?
Where is he who numbered the prisoners?
19 You will see no more of those insolent people
Who grunted in speech you could not follow,
And chattered in words you could not understand.
20 No, you shall look on Zion, our festival city!
Your eyes will see Jerusalem
Your peaceful home, a tent never to be taken down,
Whose pegs shall never be pulled up
And whose ropes shall never be broken!
21 For a glorious home shall be ours,
A place of rivers and spreading streams;
Where no ship of war is rowed
Nor stately ship is sailed.
22 For the Lord is our judge, the Lord is our ruler,
The Lord is our king; he will save us!
23 Your ropes lie slack, your flagstaff on the ground—
No need now to fly a signal of distress!
Now even the blind shares richly in the spoil,

Even the lame has time to reach his prize!
24 Now no one in the land says, I am sick,
And the people who live there will have their sins
forgiven.

CHAPTER THIRTY-FOUR

The terrible vengeance of the Lord

1 Draw near, you nations, and hear,
Listen, all you peoples!
Let the earth hear and all that fills it,
The world and all that springs from it.
2 For the Lord is angry with all nations
And his fury rages against all their armies.
He has pronounced sentence upon them,
He has marked them down for slaughter.
3 Their dead shall be flung out,
And their corpses stink to heaven
While the mountains stream with their blood.
4 The valleys shall be split open
And the skies rolled back like a scroll,
The stars will fall from heaven
As the leaf falls from the vine,
Or the withered fig from the fig-tree.
5 For my sword has drunk its fill in heaven,
Now it flashes down on Edom,
To judge a people doomed to die!
6 The sword of the Lord is clotted with blood,
It is greasy with fat—
With the blood of lambs and he-goats,
With the fat of the kidneys of rams.
For the Lord has a sacrifice in Bosrah,
A great slaughter in the land of Edom.
7 Wild oxen will fall with them,
Strong bulls and young steers together.

And their land will be soaked with blood,
Their soil enriched with fat.

Edom shall be a perpetual desert

8   For the Lord has a day of vengeance,
      A year of requital for Zion's wrongs.

9   Edom's streams shall be turned into pitch
      And her soil into sulphur;

10   The whole land shall become pitch, burning night and day,
      Which shall not be quenched forever;
      Its smoke shall go up from generation to generation,
      It shall be wasteland to all eternity,
      And no man shall ever pass through it again.

11   But the hawk and the porcupine shall possess it,
      The owl and the raven shall make their home there.
      He has measured it with the line of chaos,
      And tested it with the plummet of destruction.

12   It shall never be called a kingdom again,
      And its princes will be no more.

13   Thorns will grow over its palaces
      And thistles and nettles in its strongholds.
      It shall be a court for ostriches,

14   A rendezvous for wild cats and hyenas;
      A place where demon meets with demon,
      And there the night-hag will settle
      And find herself a resting place.

15   There shall the owl make her nest and lay,
      And hatch and gather her young in her shadow.
      Yes, there the vultures will gather together
      Each one seeking his mate.

16   (In the Lord's own book
      Not one of these is missing.[1])
      For the voice of the Lord has issued the command
      And his Spirit has brought these creatures together.

[1] The place of these words is uncertain.

17 He has allotted to them the land,
He has given it to them as their home;
There shall they live
From generation to generation.

CHAPTER THIRTY-FIVE

The glorious return to Zion

1 Let the desert and the wasteland rejoice,
2 Let the wilderness blossom with flowers of spring!
Let them exult and sing for joy
As they share the glorious growth of Lebanon,
The splendid beauty of Sharon and Carmel!
They shall see the glory of the Lord,
The majesty of our God!
3 Strengthen then the drooping hands,
Steady the trembling knees!
4 Say to the faint-hearted,
Have courage; never be afraid!
Here is your God, who comes to avenge you,
Who comes to bring recompense,
Who comes himself to save you!
5 Then shall the eyes of the blind be opened
And the ears of the deaf be unstopped;
6 Then shall the lame man leap like a stag
And the dumb man sing for joy!
For waters shall break out in the wilderness
And streams shall flow in the desert;
7 The burning sand shall become a lake
And the thirsty land bubble with water.
The lairs of jackals shall become rich meadows,
Fields of grass with reeds and rushes.
8 And there shall be in it a highway
Which shall be called the Holy Way;
No one unclean or godless may walk on it

139

And no rogue to lead men astray.
9 No lion shall be there,
   No prowling beast shall seek its prey
   Or ever be found there.
   But on this road the redeemed shall walk.
10 Those whom the Lord has ransomed shall return,
   They will come to Zion with songs on their lips,
   Their heads crowned with undying joy;
   Joy and gladness will be there to meet them
   And sorrow and sighing will be gone forever.

CHAPTERS THIRTY-SIX TO THIRTY-NINE

These chapters, which conclude the first part of the book of Isaiah, are paralleled almost exactly in 2 Kings 18.13–20.19. The chief differences in the two accounts are (a) the omission in the book of Isaiah of the story of Hezekiah's submission and payment of tribute (2 Kings 18.14–16); and (b) the addition of the psalm of thanksgiving, following Hezekiah's recovery from illness. This can be found in Isaiah 38.10–20, although most scholars do not consider this psalm to have been the work of Isaiah. The American Revised Standard Version provides a more accurate and intelligible version of the psalm than the familiar Authorised Version.

The Book of Micah

The Book of Micah

THE PROPHET. *Micah, like Amos, is a countryman. But unlike Amos he does not come from a bare desert; his home at Moresheth is green and fertile, with abundant cattle-grazing, cornfields and olive-groves. He has the sturdy independence of the man who lives on the land, and, being close to scenes of battle, he is contemptuous of those who "sit at ease in Zion" and do not see the dangers.*

Micah, delivering his message towards the end of the century, speaks for the poor, and speaks as one of them. He is horrified at the luxurious and degenerate life of the city, and realises that he and his fellow-peasants are paying for it. In another age he might have led a Peasants' Revolt, although he was no mere political agitator. It is justice, justice between men and a right attitude towards God which are his passionate concern.

THE THEME. *Micah has no political advice to offer. His message is religious and ethical, and very much down to earth. He paints a terrible picture of the decay of ordinary justice, the abuse of power by the court judges and the prevalence of bribery. He speaks of the exploitation of the poor and needy, of the rich landowners who are squeezing out those who cannot pay their exorbitant demands. Consequently there is widespread misery and degradation. The lust for money has invaded the religious sphere and even priest and prophet have grown accustomed to favouring the rich and browbeating the poor.*

Micah is red-hot with righteous indignation. He sees the evils of society not only as the heartless exploitation of the weak by the strong, but as a failure to grasp the meaning of true religion. Obedience to the laws of God is binding upon rich and poor alike, and the people to whom he is speaking have an utterly wrong idea of God. Micah's most memorable message is his famous epitome of true religion recorded in 6.8.

Yet Micah, like the other three, holds fast to the hope of an eventually purified and restored nation.

CHAPTER ONE

1 The word of the Lord which came to Micah of Moresheth when he saw the truth about Samaria and Jerusalem in the days when Jotham, Ahaz and Hezekiah were kings of Judah:

The Prophet's warning of judgement from the Lord

2 Listen, you peoples, all of you!
Let the earth and all that is in it pay heed.
For the Lord God speaks against you,
Yes, God from his holy temple.

3 See, the Lord leaves his dwelling-place
And comes down to tread upon the high places of the
earth!

4 Beneath him the mountains melt and flow into the valleys,
As wax melts before the fire and pours like water.

5 All this is because Jacob has rebelled,
And because the house of Israel has sinned.
And what is Jacob's rebellion? Surely it is Samaria!
What is the house of Judah's sin? Surely it is Jerusalem!

The Lord speaks

6 See, I am turning Samaria into a heap of stones in a field.
And I am breaking up her terraces into plots for vineyards.
Yes, I am flinging the stones of her buildings into the
valleys below,
Leaving her foundations naked and exposed.

7 All her images are smashed to pieces;

144

The shrines that she bought with her shame are burning
    in the fire,
And all that she worshipped I am utterly destroying.
For the price of her unfaithfulness pays for her betrayal!

The Prophet speaks

8   This is why I wail and lament;
    This is why I go naked and barefoot!
    I howl like a jackal and mourn like the daughters of the
        desert.
9   For Samaria has suffered a mortal blow;
    Already it strikes into Judah, and reaches to the gate of
        my own people,
    Even to Jerusalem!

*The Prophet looks at the little towns and puns
bitterly over their place-names*

10   So then, in Gath where tales are told, breathe not a word!
    In Acco, the town of Weeping, shed no tear!
    In Aphrah, the house of Dust, grovel in the dust!
11   And you who live in Shaphir, the Beauty-town, move on,
        for your shame lies naked!
    You who live in Zaanan, the town of Marching, there is
        no marching for you now!
    And Beth-ezel, standing on the hillside, can give no foot-
        hold in her sorrow,
12   The men of Maroth, that town of Bitterness, wait
        tremblingly for good,
    But disaster has come down from the Lord, to the very
        gate of Jerusalem!
13   Now, you who live in Lachish, the town far-famed for
        horses,
    Take your swiftest steeds, and hitch them to your chariots!
    For the daughter of Zion's sin began with you,

And in you was found the source of Israel's rebellion.

14 So give your farewell dowry to Moresheth of Gath!
The houses of Achzib, that dried-up brook, have proved
a delusion to the kings of Israel,

15 And once again I bring a conqueror upon you, men of
Moresheth,
While the glory of Israel is hidden away in the cave of
Adullam.

So Judah must mourn her loss

16 Make yourself bald,—yes, shave your head in sorrow for
your darling children!
Make yourself look like the bald-headed vulture,
For your children have left you and gone off into exile.

CHAPTER TWO

The Prophet condemns the wealthy in Judah

1 Woe to those who imagine wicked schemes,
Who work out evil plots while still in bed;
When daylight dawns they act—
For the power lies in their hands.

2 They covet fields and seize them.
They covet houses and take them for themselves.
They break a man and his household;
Yes, they crush him and all his rightful inheritance.

God speaks to the exploiters

3 Therefore God says,
I, the Lord, am imagining wicked schemes against this
tribe,
From which they will never be able to shake themselves
free,

Nor raise their necks in pride.
For it will be an evil time indeed!

The tables will be turned

4   When that day comes, men will taunt you,
    And sing over you this doleful dirge:
    We are utterly ruined!
    My people's land is measured off,
    It will never be ours again.
    The land is divided among our captors,
    And we are utterly ruined.

The Prophet interjects

5   So the time will come when there will be no one left
    In the congregation of the Lord
    To cast the line by lot,
    And share the land among them.

But men object to the Prophet's message

6   Never prophesy like that,
    (But a prophet must prophesy!)
    'No man should prophesy such things!
    (Disaster, you see, can never come upon them!)
7   Listen, you who speak like this to the house of Jacob!
    Has the Lord grown short in temper?
    Would he ever perform such actions as these?
    Are not his words full of kindness to those who walk
        uprightly?

The Prophet replies

8   But you have become my people's enemies,
    You make war against men of peace.

You steal the robes from quiet passers-by,
Whose thoughts are far from war.

9   You drive women from their happy homes,
And condemn their children to hopeless slavery.

10   Get up and get out!
You are trespassing here;
The land is befouled,
And for this it is doomed
To irrevocable disaster!

The Prophet comments

11   The sort of prophet this people wants is a windbag and a
        liar,
Prophesying a future of "wines and spirits"!

God speaks of events after the judgement

12   I will most surely gather you all together again, O Jacob;
I will most surely bring home the survivors of Israel.
I will bring them all together like sheep into a fold,
A crowd of men noisy as a flock in its pasture.

13   Their leader has broken out, they have opened a gap;
They have passed through the gate and gone out by it!
Their king shall proceed before them,
With the Lord at the head of them all.

CHAPTER THREE

The Prophet denounces the leaders and rulers

1   Then I said,
    Listen, now, you leaders of Jacob,
    And rulers of the house of Israel!
    Are you not the guardians of justice?
2   Yes, you who hate the good and love the evil!
    You tear the hide off my people,
3   You tear the flesh from their bones.
    You eat the flesh of my people,
    You rip off their skin.
    You break their bones and chop them into pieces,
    Like meat in a cooking-pot,
    Like flesh stewing in a cauldron.

Disaster will come to them

4   The day will come when they will cry to the Lord,
    But he will not heed them.
    At that time he will hide his face from them,
    Because of their evil deeds.

The Prophet denounces the false prophets

5   As for the prophets that lead my people astray—
    Those who cry, Peace, so long as their mouths are full
    But declare war against them who will not feed them—
    The Lord says this:
6   It shall be night for you, night without vision.
    You shall know darkness in which you can divine nothing!
    The sun shall set upon the prophets,
7   And their day shall end in darkness.
    The seers shall be disgraced,

And the diviners openly shamed.
All of them will hold their hands over their mouths,
For no answer comes from God.

The Prophet himself is strong in the truth

8 But as for me, I am filled with power
Through the Spirit of the Lord!
I can see what is just and right,
And I have the strength to declare it,
To tell Jacob plainly of his transgression,
And Israel of his sin.

9 Listen to this, you leaders of Jacob,
And rulers of the house of Israel,
You who hate what is right and twist what is straight;

10 Who build Zion with bloodshed, and Jerusalem with
crime.

11 Her leaders dispense justice—at a price,
Her priests teach—what they are paid to teach,
And her prophets see visions—according to the fees they
receive.
Yet they rest happily upon the Lord and say,
Is not the Lord in our midst?
No disaster could ever strike us.

12 Therefore, it is because of you
That Zion shall be ploughed up like a field,
Jerusalem shall become a heap of ruins;
And the mount of the temple shall be
A tangle of scrub on the top of a hill.

CHAPTER FOUR

The Prophet looks at the far horizon

1 In the last days it will come to pass
That the mountain of the Lord
Shall tower above the peaks,
Lifted high above the hills,
And peoples shall swarm to it!
2 Great nations will arrive and say,
Come, let us go up to the mountain of the Lord,
And to the house of the God of Jacob.
He will give us knowledge of his ways,
And we will follow in his paths.
For the Law goes forth from Zion,
And the Word of the Lord from Jerusalem.

The Lord will rule over all nations in peace

3 And he will judge between great peoples,
And make decision between nations far and wide.
Then they shall hammer their swords into ploughshares,
And their spears into pruning-hooks.
Nation shall lift no sword against nation,
And never again will they learn to make war.
4 Every man shall live beneath the shade of his own vine
and fig-tree,
And no one shall make him afraid.
The Lord of hosts has declared this with his own voice!

The Prophet's interjection

For now the peoples walk each in the name of their gods,
But as for us, we will walk in the name of the Lord our
God for ever!

4. THE BOOK OF MICAH

The promise of the Lord

6   In that day, the Lord declares,
    I will gather up the crippled,
    And bring in the outcast and those whom I have afflicted.
7   I will make the disabled the stock of the future,
    And a strong nation of those who are sick.
    And the Lord will reign over them in Mount Zion,
    From this time onwards, and for ever!

The Prophet speaks of the future—

8   And you, the Watch-tower of the flock,
    Hill-fortress of the daughter of Zion,
    To you shall return the rule of former time,
    And the kingdom shall be restored to the daughter of
        Jerusalem.

—and of the terrible present

9   Why are you now broken to pieces? Have you no king?
    Is your counsellor dead?
    Is that why pangs have seized you
    Like a woman in the pains of childbirth?
10 Yes, you may well writhe and groan, daughter of Zion,
    Like a woman in labour.
    For now you must leave the city
    To make your camp in the fields,
    And go far away to Babylon.
    But it is there that you will be rescued,
    And it is there that the Lord will set you free from the
        hand of your enemies.

The present danger and future victory

11 Now, great nations are gathered against you and they say,
    Let her be defiled that we may feast our eyes upon Zion.

12 But they do not know the thoughts of the Lord,
Nor do they understand his plan.
For he will collect them up
Like sheaves for the threshing floor.

13 So, arise and thresh, daughter of Zion!
I will give you horns of iron and hoofs as hard as bronze.
And you shall trample down great nations,
Giving their yield to the Lord,
Their riches to the Lord of the whole earth.

CHAPTER FIVE

Jerusalem's present peril at the hands of Assyria

1 Now call up your troops, you daughter of troops!
For the siege is laid against us,
And in insult they will take a stick,
And strike the judge of Israel on the cheek!

Nevertheless, the Messiah will surely come

2 But you, Bethlehem Ephratah,
Almost too small to be counted
Among the ranks of Judah,
From you shall come forth for me
The future Ruler of Israel!
He springs from a line of ancient times,
From the days of long ago.

God's apparent neglect

3 Therefore, the Lord leaves them to themselves,
Until the time when she who is in labour
Has given birth to her child.
Until the rest of his brethren have returned
With the children of Israel.

4   Then he shall stand as their Shepherd
Firm in the strength of the Lord,
In the majesty of the name of the Lord his God.
And they shall come in and possess the land,
Because he will be great
To the very ends of the earth.

Trust in eventual victory

5   This shall deliver us from the Assyrian
When he invades our land,
And marches over our borders.
We will raise against him seven shepherds
And eight princes of men.

6   They will look after the land of Assyria with a sword,
And care for the land of Nimrod with a naked blade!
They shall deliver us from the Assyrian
When he invades our land,
And marches over our borders.

Israel's survivors will prove both a blessing—

7   Then the survivors of Jacob
Shall be among many peoples
Like dew from the Lord,
Like showers upon the grass,
Which never wait for men,
Nor linger for the sons of men.

—and a destructive force

8   Yes, the survivors of Jacob
Shall live among many nations,
Like a lion among the beasts of the jungle,
As a young lion among the flocks of sheep;
Who treads down and tears in pieces,

As he makes his way along,
And there is none to defend them!

The Prophet reassures—

9   Yes, your hand shall be lifted up above your adversaries,
And all your enemies shall be destroyed.

—but the Lord will destroy what is evil

10   In that day, says the Lord,
I will destroy your horses,
And I will break up your chariots.

11   I will demolish the cities of your land
And lay your strongholds in ruin.

12   I will shatter the witchcraft you hold in your hand,
And you shall have no more peerers into the clouds

13   I will also break down your graven images,
And the pillars which stand in your midst.
No longer shall you worship the work of your hands.

14   I will tear out your sacred groves by the roots,
And I will utterly destroy your idols.

15   So will I execute vengeance in wrath and anger
Upon the nations who do not obey me.

CHAPTER SIX

The Lord's case against his people

1   Listen now to the word
Which the Lord has spoken;
Get up and plead your cause before the mountains,
And let the hills hear your voice.

2   Hear, you mountains, the complaint of the Lord,
And listen, you deep-laid foundations of the earth!
For the Lord has a case against his people,
And brings his argument against Israel:

6. THE BOOK OF MICAH

The Lord speaks

3 My people, what have I ever done to you?
   How have I ever brought you down? Tell me!
4 Did I not bring you up out of the land of Egypt?
   Did I not set you free from the house of slavery?
   It was I who sent Moses, Aaron and Miriam to lead you.
5 Remember, my people, what Balak, King of Moab,
      planned,
   Remember how Balaam, son of Beor, answered him!
   Remember all that happened from Shittim to Gilgal,
   That you may be sure that the Lord is strong to save.

The exaggeration of the "religious" approach—

6 How shall I come into the presence of the Lord,
   And bow myself low before the most high God?
   Shall I approach him with burnt-offerings—with calves a
      full year old?
7 Will the Lord be pleased with thousands of rams,
   With ten thousand rivers of oil?
   Shall I give my first-born to pay for my own misdeeds—
   The fruit of my flesh for the sin of my soul?

—is brought down to earth by the Prophet

8 You know well enough, Man, what is good!
   For what does the Lord require from you,
   But to be just, to love mercy,
   And to walk humbly with your God?

The Lord's urgent words

9 Listen! The voice of the Lord cries out to the city,
   (And it is wise to revere his name):

6. THE BOOK OF MICAH

Hear this, you people and council of the city!
10　Can I forget the ill-gotten hoards in the houses of wicked
　　　men?
　　Can I forget the infamous practice of giving short measure?
11　How can I consider a man pure with his loaded balances
　　And his bag of false weights?
12　The rich among you are full of violence,
　　Your citizens are liars every one.

The Lord's judgement is an inevitable consequence

13　Therefore I will begin my attack upon you,
　　And will bring you down to ruin for your sins;
14　You will eat but you will not be satisfied,
　　For there will be famine in your heart.
　　You may store, but you will never save,
　　And what you save I will surrender to the sword.
15　You will sow, but you will not reap;
　　You will tread the olives, but you will not anoint your-
　　　selves with oil.
　　You will tread the grapes, but you will not drink the wine.
16　For you are walking by the rules of Omri,
　　And aping the ways of the house of Ahab.
　　These are the counsels which you have followed,
　　And they compel me to bring you to ruin,
　　And make your inhabitants an object of scorn,
　　So that you become the laughing-stock of all peoples.

CHAPTER SEVEN

Jerusalem laments her state: honesty is gone

1 Alas for me, for I have become
Like a bare orchard or a stripped vine.
There is not a bunch of grapes left to eat—
Not a single ripe fig to satisfy my longing.

2 Good-living men have vanished from the land,
And no true man remains among them!
They all lurk, with murder in their hearts,
Every man hunts his brother to catch him in a net.

3 Their hands are ready for evil and their hearts are set upon
it.
The ruler and the judge demand their price;
The great man makes no secret of his desires.
So they weave their life together—

4 The best of them like a tangled briar,
And the straightest among them more twisted than a hedge
of thorn.

Terrible punishment is inevitable

4b The day which the watchers foresaw,
The day of punishment, has come;
Now follows utter destruction.

Confidence has been destroyed

5 Have no faith in your neighbour;
Do not trust your closest friend;
Share no secret with your wife.

6 For the son treats his father with contempt,
And the daughter defies her mother,
The daughter-in-law rebels against her mother-in-law,
And a man's enemies are those of his own household.

158

7. THE BOOK OF MICAH

A psalm of confidence in the Lord

7   But as for me, my eyes look for the Lord.
    I will wait for the God who will save me;
    Yes, my God will deliver me!
8   Never exult over me, my enemy—
    When I fall, I shall rise again;
    When I sit in darkness,
    The Lord shall be my light.
9   I will endure the displeasure of the Lord,
    (For I have sinned against him),
    Until the day when he takes up my cause,
    And vindicates my right.
    He will bring me out into the light,
    And I shall see the justness of his ways.

Israel's vindication and her enemies' discomfiture

10 My enemy will see it too;
    She, who said to me,
    Where is the Lord your God?
    Shall be covered with shame.
    My eyes will gloat over her,
    For she will be trampled down
    Like mud in the streets.

Israel shall be restored

11 That day shall be the day for the building of your
        walls,
    The day for far-flung boundaries;
12 The day when peoples shall come to you,
    From Assyria to Egypt,
    And from Egypt to the great River,
    From sea to sea, from mountain to mountain.

13   For their lands will be waste-lands because of the inhabitants,
Whose deeds have borne the fruit of desolation.

The Prophet prays to the Lord

14   Shepherd your people, your own flock, O Lord, with
your staff[1]
For they live lonely in the desert—with rich fields all
around them.
Let their pasture be in Bashan and Gilead, as in the days
of old.

15   Give us wonders to see, as in the days when you came
out of Egypt!

For all nations shall see his power

16   May the nations see and be ashamed of all their
strength.
Let them put their hands to their mouths; let their ears be
deafened.

17   May they lick the dust like serpents, like the worms of the
earth.
May they come trembling out of their hiding-places,
And cower in fear before the Lord our God.

The Prophet addresses the Lord in complete trust

18   Where else is a God like you, who forgives transgression
and passes over wrong?
For the sake of his people's survivors he does not store
his anger for ever,
But delights in showing mercy.

19   He will come back, he will pity us,
He will trample our sins under his feet.
Yes, you will cast all our sins into the depths of the sea;

20   You will show your faithfulness to Jacob, your true love
      to Abraham,
      As you have sworn to our fathers, from the days of long
      ago.

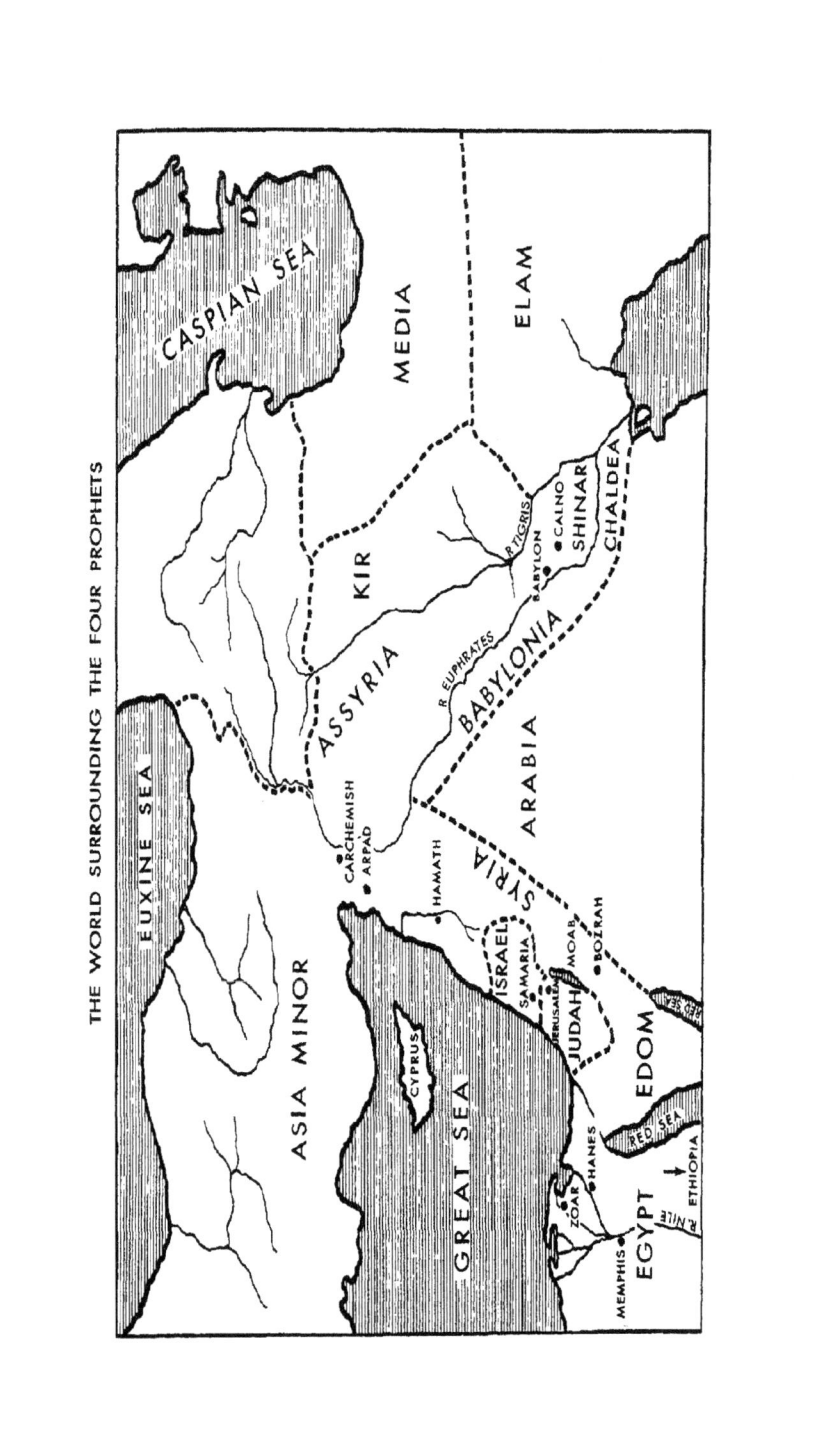

THE LAND IN THE TIME OF THE FOUR PROPHETS

CPSIA information can be obtained
at www.ICGtesting.com
Printed in the USA
BVHW041435050919
557674BV00003B/103/P